Games, Ideas and Activities for Early Years Mathematics

Other titles in the series

Barron: Practical Ideas, Games and Activities for the Primary Classroom

Drinkwater: Games and Activities for Primary Modern Foreign Languages

Allen: Games, Ideas and Activities for Primary PE

Dabell: Games, Ideas and Activities for Primary Mathematics

Coulson and Cousins: Games, Ideas and Activities for Early Years Phonics

Minto: Games, Ideas and Activities for Primary Music

Green: Games, Ideas and Activities for Primary Humanities

Barron: Games, Ideas and Activities for Learning Outside the Primary Classroom

Labrow: Creative Activities for the Secondary Classroom

Theodorou: Games, Ideas and Activities for Primary Drama

Glynne and Snowden: Games, Ideas and Activities for Primary Literacy

Dabell: Games, Ideas and Activities for Primary Science

Cousins: Games, Ideas and Activities for Early Years Literacy

Bower: Games, Ideas and Activities for Primary Poetry

Webster: Creative Activities and Ideas for Pupils with English as an Additional Language

Games, Ideas and Activities for Early Years Mathematics

Alice Hansen

Longman
is an imprint of

Harlow, England • London • New York • Boston • San Francisco • Toronto
Sydney • Tokyo • Singapore • Hong Kong • Seoul • Taipei • New Delhi
Cape Town • Madrid • Mexico City • Amsterdam • Munich • Paris • Milan

PEARSON EDUCATION LIMITED
Edinburgh Gate
Harlow CM20 2JE
Tel: +44 (0)1279 623623
Fax: +44 (0)1279 431059
Website: www.pearson.com/uk

First published in Great Britain in 2012

ISBN: 978-1-4082-8484-1

British Library Cataloguing-in-Publication Data
A catalogue record for this book is available from the British Library

Library of Congress Cataloging-in-Publication Data
A catalog record for this book is available from the Library of Congress

10 9 8 7 6 5 4 3 2
15 14

Cartoon illustrations by Cathy Hughes
Typeset in 8.5 pt News Gothic by 3
Printed and bound in Malaysia (CTP-PPSB)

Contents

Introduction

Aimee: 'I live at number 4.'
Ashmal: 'I live at number 12.'
Jake: 'Well, I live at number 73.'
Kate: 'I live at 106.'
Aimee: 'Well, I live at number thousand!'
Jake: 'I live at one million!'
(All laugh)

I overheard the above in a nursery recently. The four three-year-old children were standing together on the carpet and Aimee instigated the conversation. What struck me the most was the way that the children joined in spontaneously, understood the numbers were increasing and shared Aimee's and Jake's humour of living at ludicrous addresses.

This is only one little snapshot of the mathematical talk and play that can be seen in early years settings every day. All young children intuitively use number and other mathematical concepts continuously in their play, and take great pleasure in doing so. The key for practitioners and teachers is to plan activities, games and tasks that are mathematical in nature as well as to see the mathematical opportunities in many of the everyday activities that happen in a setting or classroom.

This is a book of practical ideas, games and activities written for children in the early years stages, aged four to five. However, because of its broad nature, much of the content will also be suitable for younger children as well as most six year-olds. You will notice that some of the themes in this book are addressed in other books in the series. This was planned intentionally so that you can take advantage of the themes across several areas of learning. Each activity contains the following sections:

Title

The title provides the theme of the activities (such as 'pirates'), the resources used (such as 'dice') or the mathematical concepts (such as 'number') that the activities, games and ideas relate to in that section.

Aims and objectives

This provides general statements related to the main focuses of the activity.

Resources

A list of the resources you will need is given. Some resources are optional and these are marked clearly.

Preparation

This outlines any preparation that is required over and above gathering the resources.

What to do

This section provides a step-by-step guide to the activity, outlining what you and the children will be doing.

Tip(s)

Tips may be related to the organisation of the activity, resources that can be used, how to engage the children further or what mathematical ideas to focus upon specifically.

Variation(s)

This gives ideas for how the activity can be amended to suit other themes, or developed to extend the original ideas.

How is this maths?

This section explains why the activity is mathematical and how the ideas develop into primary school mathematics and beyond.

Most of the ideas in this book can be adapted for a wide range of themes, so please look through the whole book for inspiration rather than focusing only on a particular theme you may be teaching.

This book includes, but also goes beyond, problem-solving, reasoning and numeracy in curriculum guidance. It creates space for children to explore 'big ideas' in maths, such as infinity and large numbers that excite and amaze. And it introduces ideas of how children's mathematical development can be supported in the early years. Use these games, ideas and activities as a springboard for identifying mathematical opportunities present in all your early years provision. With the aid of this book, it is hoped that you will then be able to move beyond the ideas presented here.

About the author

Dr Alice Hansen taught in England and abroad until moving into Early Years and Primary Initial Teacher Education at St Martin's College, University of Cumbria. She left higher education to become an educational consultant. During that time she worked with a number of educational settings and national bodies, focusing on continuing professional development for teachers in mathematics education. She is now the director of Children Count Ltd, a company that provides a range of consultancy, research and publications for early years and primary educational settings.

Chapter 1
Dressing Up

Introduction

Dressing up is an activity enjoyed by all children. This chapter contains activities that can be undertaken in the dress shop role-play area. Alternatively, you may place the clothes in a suitcase for the children to talk about and try on. Remember to include a wide range of types of clothes and jewellery from different cultures.

In the clothes shop

Use the role-play area as a clothes shop to facilitate mathematical discussion.

Can we match it?

Practise 1-to-1 correspondence by finding colours that are the same

Aims and objectives

- To identify colours accurately.
- To group objects according to their colour.

Preparation

- Gather selections of girls' and boys' clothing and accessories that have the same colour. These may be clothes, shoes, hats or bags that the children can wear, available in the role-play clothing shop.

What to do

- Open the role-play clothes shop, inviting a small number of children to browse in your new shop.
- Explain to the children that you had a visitor yesterday who bought only green items and you noticed how smart they looked when everything they wore matched.
- Ask the children if they can select items that are all the same colour.
- Discuss why they have chosen the items they have. Focus discussion on the similar properties of the items (they are all the same colour). Also discuss how they are different.

You may want to produce cards with colours that match the sets you have created for the children to choose, to help them match the colours and to avoid children selecting the same colour.

Variation

If it is not possible to use the role-play area for this activity, a smaller-scale activity could be to have items for the dolls and teddies to wear, or to use drawings copied onto various colours of paper for children to stick on their sheets.

How is this maths?

Being able to identify characteristics (attributes) of objects (and later numbers) is important for children to be able to group them. This lays a foundation for them being able to handle data later on. Matching colour also helps children to practise 1-to-1 correspondence.

Putting on and putting away our clothes

Thinking about the use of positional language while wearing and tidying away the clothes in the role play shop.

Aims and objectives

- To use positional language.
- To use ordinal language.
- To compare size.

What to do

- While the children are trying clothes on, talk to them about what they are doing. Reinforce positional language such as 'on', 'in', 'over', 'under', 'through'. E.g. 'Place the hat *on* your head, put your arm *through* the sleeve, the jacket is *over* the shirt'.
- While the children are putting away clothes, talk to them about the position or place of the clothes. E.g. 'The clothes are *in* the drawer, the dress is *on* the hanger, the shoes are *in* the box'.
- While the children are putting clothes on, talk to them about the size of the clothing. 'Is this top *too big, too small,* or *just right*?'
- Talk to the children about the order they put their clothes on. E.g. socks on *first*, shoes on *second*.

Once you have modelled this language, step back and observe the children taking on the role of shopkeeper and using this language themselves!

How is this maths?

Using positional language and talking about size helps children to make sense of shape and space and supports their geometrical thinking. Using ordinal language helps children to think about order and is another way of thinking about numbers. Comparing size helps children to make sense of shape and measurement.

How much?

An opportunity for children to buy and sell clothes in the clothes shop.

Aims and objectives

- To use language associated with money.
- To handle coins and notes.

Preparation

- Install a till in the role play clothing shop.
- Place price labels on the clothes. You may work with some children to create the labels from scratch.

What to do

- Open the shop, with two children as the proprietors. Encourage the children to read the cost of the item and to charge the customer the amount for the item.
- The children can take money and give change, or use a credit card for the transaction!
- The children may make discount vouchers to encourage customers to return.

You will need to think about the amounts that you put on the items in the shop. Some people believe that the amounts should be small and in pence, for children to read and handle coins accurately. Others believe that the amounts on the items should be more realistic because it would not be possible to find a pair of gloves for 5p. Talk with your colleagues about which approach you will take.

Variation

The children may use a calculator or the till to add up the cost of several items.

How is this maths?

It is important that children handle money and learn to recognise the value of coins. Children find understanding the value of coins difficult. Coins of different values are different sizes (for example a 5p is worth more than a 2p, but a 2p is larger). A one-pound coin is the equivalent of one hundred pence, but is represented by only one coin.

Making necklaces

Making necklaces is a fun way to talk about patterns and order together.

Aims and objectives

- To copy or create a repeating pattern.
- To use ordinal language (first, second, third and so on).

Resources

- Beads, buttons, pasta or similar for threading
- String or wool
- Selection of necklaces or bracelets (bought or made from beads) from role play

Preparation

- Set out the materials in containers. You may wish to separate colours for younger children.

What to do

- Begin to make a necklace using two alternating colours (A,B,A,B: e.g. red, blue, red, blue, red, blue . . .). Ask the children what they notice.
- Can the children tell you what comes next? What would the next two beads be? What about the next three? Can they make it?
- Begin another, using two colours in a pattern (AAB, AAB: e.g. red, red, blue, red, red, blue . . .). Ask the children what they notice.
- Can the children tell you what comes next? What would the next two beads be? What about the next three? Can they make it?
- Ask the children to create their own necklace. Can they make a repeating pattern on their necklace?

- **Start with two colours only. Young children find using more than two or three very difficult.**
- **Necklaces can be tedious to complete as they are long. Use large beads, or make smaller necklaces for the teddies, or bracelets instead.**

Variation

Print patterns on paper using different-coloured shapes. Cut the paper out to dress the paper doll.

How is this maths?

Mathematics is full of pattern. Seeing pattern helps children to solve problems. Being able to say what comes next helps children to visualise shape or colour and pattern. Using ordinal language (first, second, etc.) helps them to talk mathematically.

Designing clothes

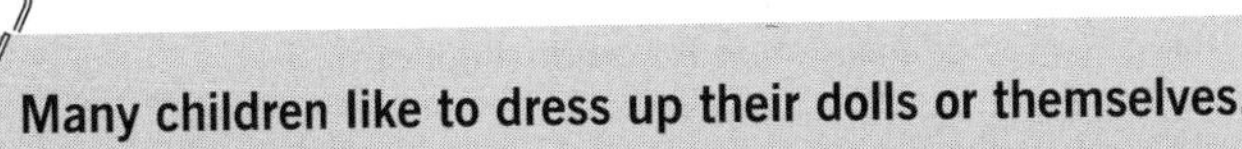

Many children like to dress up their dolls or themselves.

Aims and objectives

- To construct using materials.
- To estimate length.

Resources

- Lengths of material – use as wide a range of fabrics as possible
- Ribbon
- Scissors
- Sticky tape
- Photographs of children in clothes (optional)

Preparation

- Set out the materials available to the children.

What to do

- Encourage the children to think about creating their own clothes.
- Talk to them about which clothes they are going to make, and discuss the suitability of the material for the purpose of that clothing.
- Talk with the children about how much fabric they will need to create their clothes. Do they have enough? Is it wide enough? Too long? How do they know? How are they going to find out? What will they do to resolve any problems about the size of the fabric?
- What order will they need to follow to create their clothes?
- Whom will they work with?

- Children may find it easier to create an item of clothing for their friend.
- You may wish to photograph the children in their creations and display them to provide inspiration for other children.

Variation

Make a costume for a new superhero. How will the costume help them use their super powers?

How is this maths?

Children who use estimation are able to check the accuracy of their work more effectively. The children will develop their understanding of length by using arbitrary units of length (e.g. about a child's height) and standard measures (e.g. a metre stick) to become more accurate in their measuring.

Chapter 2
Oh, we do like to be beside the seaside!

Introduction

Playing with the resources in this theme offers children opportunities to experiment with different textures. You can transform all the available space into a seaside setting if you want to explore these on a grand scale, or alternatively utilise these activities in the sand and water area.

Sand and water

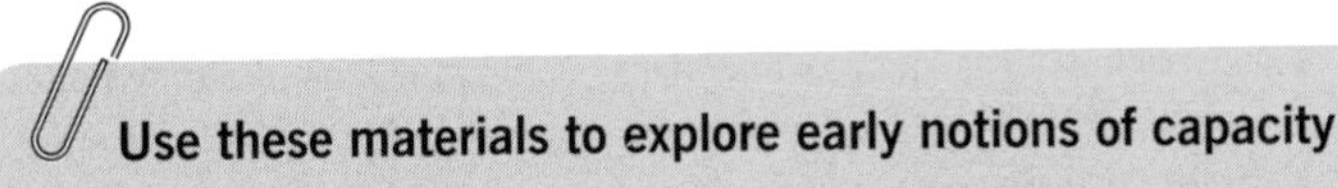

Aims and objectives

- To fill, empty and compare buckets.

Resources

- Large tarpaulin or paddling pool
- Dry sand
- Water tray
- Buckets of different sizes
- Spades and other items to scoop sand and water
- Funnels, sieves, etc. to let sand and water through

Preparation

- Lay the tarpaulin or the pool on the floor or outside and fill with the sand.
- Fill the water tray.

What to do

- Talk with the children about which bucket holds more/less. Discuss ways they could test this. Try pouring from one bucket to another. Does this help?
- What about three containers? Can they order them from which one holds most to least? How can they see if they are right?
- Use words describing how much water or dry sand is in the bucket, such as full, empty, half full, nearly full, as well as talking about what the children are doing. E.g. 'I see you are filling it up, are you going to add some more to fill it up? How many scoops do you think will fill this bucket? What about this bucket?'

Tips

- **Colouring water with food colouring helps children to see the level of the water in the containers more easily.**
- **Conservation of capacity is a very difficult idea for young children. Select buckets of all shapes and sizes. Some may look like they hold more because they are taller but actually they hold less because they are thinner! Researchers say children need lots of experience using different-shaped containers to help them understand conservation of capacity.**

How is this maths?

This activity supports children's early development of capacity. It also encourages them to think about how space is filled and how containers of different shapes may have the same, or different, capacities.

Sandcastles

Use an array of containers to construct sandcastles.

Aims and objectives

- To construct sandcastles.
- To decorate sandcastles.

Resources

- Large tarpaulin or paddling pool
- Damp sand
- Buckets of different sizes
- Spades and other items to scoop sand
- Shells, driftwood and other items found at the beach
- Pictures of sandcastles (optional)

Preparation

- Lay the tarpaulin or the pool on the floor and fill with the damp sand.
- Make a sandcastle to leave on the sand for the children to find.

What to do

- Ask the children if any of them have made a sandcastle before. If they have, ask them to demonstrate how they made it. Encourage them to talk about what they are doing during each step in the process. Reinforce any mathematical vocabulary they are using (e.g. put sand *in* the bucket, pat the sand *down*, tip the bucket *upside down*).
- Talk about how they can make sandcastles with more than one storey. Discuss the size of the different storeys. Which bucket might they use first? Why?
- Decorate sandcastles with shells, driftwood, flags, etc. Can they make a pattern that repeats around the outside of the sandcastle?

The amount of water that is added to the sand is important to get right. Sand that is too dry or too wet will not keep its shape. Try making sandcastles yourself before the children arrive so you know it works.

How is this maths?

Making sandcastles requires a lot of problem solving, especially when the sandcastles fail to stand up the first time! Children need to think about the reason why their sandcastle did not stand up, and think logically about how they could improve their attempt the next time. Using trial and error is an effective problem-solving approach in the early years and beyond.

Beach towels

Let's use our beach towels on the beach!

Aims and objectives

- To sort according to common criteria.
- To compare sizes.

Resources

- A variety of beach towels in different sizes, including one as large as possible

Preparation

- Pile the towels in the middle of the floor, all mixed up.

What to do

- Ask the children to sit in a circle around the towels.
- Explain that you found this pile of towels on the beach and you want to find out more about them. Ask the children what they might want to find out about them.
- Children's responses will vary, and be positive about each one. However, for the purposes of this activity focus on the responses that are more mathematical, such as colour, pattern and size.
- Choose one of the ideas (such as colour) and ask the children to come up in turn and choose a towel, sorting it according to the criterion (characteristic). Discuss the number of towels in each group.
- Identify the biggest towel (this may have been spotted as the children were dismantling the pile). See how many children can fit on the towel, either standing on it or lying on it.

- Ask who thinks they sorted the smallest towel. You are likely to get a number of children thinking their towel was the smallest. Discuss how they can check which is the smallest. Count the number of children who can stand or lie on this towel. Compare, using language such as *more* and *less*.
- Repeat with other towels, ordering them in size. Discuss how this is different from ordering them in order of length only.

Conservation of area is a very difficult idea for young children. Select towels of all shapes and sizes. Some may look like they are bigger because they are longer but actually they have a smaller area because they are thinner! Researchers say children need lots of experience using different-shaped areas to help them understand conservation of area.

Variations

- Children can compare the area of different paper shapes by covering the shapes in counters, cubes or other items.
- Can the children cover the floor with the towels, without overlapping and without leaving gaps?

How is this maths?

This supports children's early understanding of area. By seeing the towels in different orientations, and talking about the size of the shapes, early understanding of the notion of quadrilaterals is also developing.

The tide

This activity explores a pattern as old as the Earth.

Aims and objectives

- To understand how the tide moves in and out of the beach twice a day.

Resources

- Children's picture book about the tide (e.g. *Once Upon a Tide* by Tony Mitton and Selina Young; *High Tide, Low Tide* by Mick Manning and Brita Granstrom; *In Comes the Tide* by Valerie King)
- Long length of blue or white chiffon or similar fabric

Preparation

- Read the picture book

What to do

- Discuss how the tide moves in and out, and the impact that this has on the creatures etc. in the book or on their own experiences of visiting the beach (if appropriate).
- Talk about the timing of the tide and that it rises and falls around twice a day.
- Ask the children to choose to be one of the creatures (or other appropriate item) from the book. Two adults hold the fabric and pretend that the fabric is the tide rising and falling while the children act out being the creature.
- Discuss what they did when they were the creature. What impact does the tide have on their life? What do they do when it is high tide? Or low tide? Why?
- What would happen if the tide remained low, or high?

How is this maths?

The tide is one example of a naturally occurring pattern. (High tide tends to occur approximately twice a day, but is actually on a 24-hour 50-minute cycle, so it takes place 50 minutes later each day.) Understanding the repetitive nature of patterns is a fundamental mathematical understanding.

The rock pool

Exploring the creatures in the rock pool always excites children and adults like!

Aims and objectives

- To discuss the features belonging to rock pool inhabitants.
- To sort creatures according to their attributes.

Resources

- Water tray
- Rocks
- Sand
- Plastic creatures such as sea slugs, shrimps, crabs, sea eggs, fish, small octopus, snails
- Plastic seaweed such as neptune's necklace, sea lettuce

Preparation

- Set up the water tray to re-create a rock pool.
- Hide various plastic rock pool creatures and plants in a typical resting place.

What to do

- Encourage the children to explore the rock pool.
- As a find is made, encourage the children to describe the features of the creature.
- Can they sort the creatures in any way? Consider thinking about the patterns on their bodies, the number of legs or methods of movement under the water or overland.

Use ice-cream containers with labels the children have designed themselves to sort the creatures. These will contain the water and allow the children to look at the sets more easily.

Variations

- As an extension the children may sort using two criteria: where would the children's creatures belong in the Carroll diagram below?

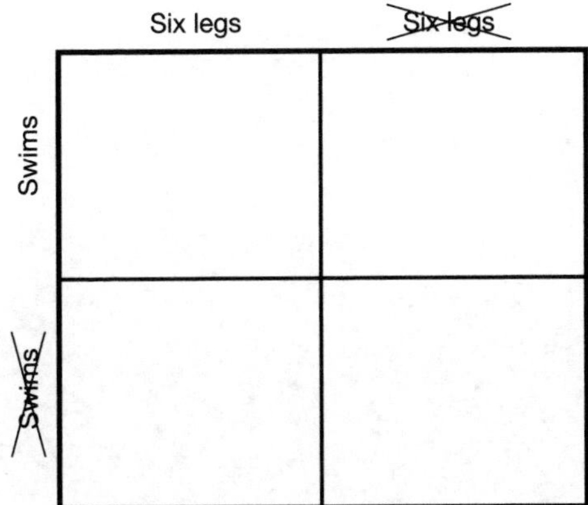

- You may visit a real rock pool. Remember that rock pools are very fragile environments for a number of creatures and it is essential that the children take great care when exploring them.

How is this maths?

Identifying the features of the creatures may involve counting, or observing pattern. Being able to sort items into categories is within the early stages of handling data.

Chapter 3
Space

Introduction

In addition to the activities in this chapter, you might want to set up a small, darkened area in the room that has been constructed using thick black polythene sheeting. In this area the children can use torches to explore objectives that reflect, and look at the stars in the 'sky' at the top. To make a star-filled sky effect you can glue glitter onto the top of the area or use twinkling low-energy Christmas lights.

Blast off!

Enjoy blasting off with the rockets!

Aims and objectives

- To count backwards in steps of one.
- To follow simple instructions.

Resources

- Mission control centre (this could be anything from the role-play area to a decorated box on the tabletop)
- Rocket(s) made by the children, or toy rockets

Preparation

- Identify who will be ground control and who will be the astronaut taking the rocket into space.

What to do

- Count down from 3, 5 or 10 for the rocket to 'blast off'.
- Take turns being at ground control and being the astronaut.

Variations

- Vary the starting number. Ask the children what number they would like to start with!
- There are many different contexts in which the children can count down – they may count down to dinner, to start a race or to pop up like a jack-in-the-box.

How is this maths?

Children need to be able to count forwards and backwards. Later on they will do this in steps other than ones. Waiting until a given time (in this case 'blast off') helps children to follow instructions and gain an appreciation of time as duration.

Rocket construction

Choose three-dimensional figures to make a rocket.

Aims and objectives

- To construct a rocket that will stand and fly.
- To consider the features of three-dimensional shapes.

Resources

- Construction materials
- Pictures or video material of rockets or toy rockets

What to do

- Show the children a range of rockets. Discuss the purpose of the rockets and the features that help them to achieve their purpose.
- Ask the children what shapes they are going to use/are using to construct their rocket. Talk to them about why that shape is a good shape to use (e.g. the cone has a point that helps it to travel through space).

Model the correct three-dimensional language, such as cone, cylinder, cuboid, cube.

How is this maths?

Children learn about shape and space by manipulating construction materials. Helping them to think about the features of the shapes enables them to develop an early understanding of geometric definition.

To infinity and beyond!

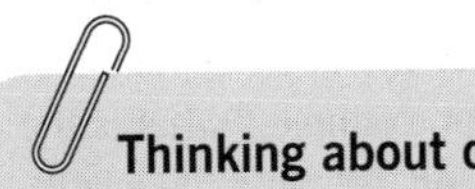

Thinking about distance and perspective in space.

Aims and objectives

- To consider how distance affects the size of things we can see.
- To use language related to size and distance/length.

Resources

- Two balls of differing sizes, e.g. one football and one golf ball
- Large field or long room

Preparation

- Ask another adult to stand as far away as possible holding a large ball. (The actual size of the ball will depend on how far the adult can move away from the children.)

What to do

- Talk about rockets, and where they travel. Where would the children like their rocket to travel to? Talk about the distances being a very long way (or not, as the case may be!) from the Earth.
- Ask the children to find the adult who is holding the ball at a distance. What ball do they think they are holding? Exclaim to the children that they can't be right (if they have guessed the ball correctly), because you are holding this (small) ball here and it seems larger than the ball the adult is holding. Discuss why this might be happening.
- Ask the adult to return. Encourage the children to observe what happens to the mystery ball as the adult comes closer. Compare the two balls side by side.
- Talk about the Earth being spherical, a giant ball-shaped planet floating in space, and how the sun is many, many times bigger than the Earth but it appears very small in the sky because it is a very long way from us.

How is this maths?

By observing the sizes of the balls at a distance and closely, children have an opportunity to talk about how distance has an effect on our perception of objects. Distance is another way to describe length. For example, 'What is the distance between points A and B?' is the same as asking, 'What is the length between points A and B?'. Talking about large distances in space can also lead children to thinking about the notion of *infinity*.

Stars

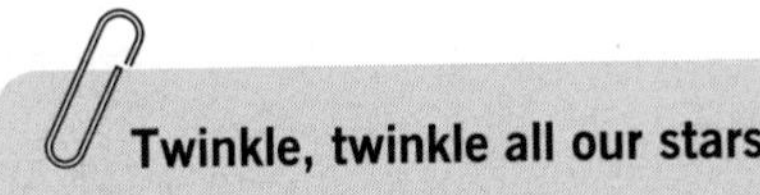

Aims and objectives

- To count a set of points.

Resources

- Cardboard
- Glitter, paint or coloured paper pieces for decoration

Preparation

- Cut out a variety of stars, with different numbers of points:

What to do

- Encourage the children to choose and decorate some stars. While doing so, urge them to count the number of points that the stars have.
- Talk with each other about the number of points.
- Display the stars by hanging them from the ceiling.

You may need to help the children to remember what point they have started counting from and therefore which point to stop counting at. Often young children will keep counting around, or stop at a number that is familiar to them (often 10). Using a finger to identify where the counting has begun is one way.

Variation

Encourage the children to draw and/or cut out their own shapes with the number of points that they want.

How is this maths?

Knowing that the last number stated in a counting sequence gives the cardinal (total) number of items in the set is part of young children's development of counting.

Star symmetry

Exploring symmetry through order of rotation and reflection.

Aims and objectives

- To recognise symmetry.

Resources

- Variety of stars cut out of cardboard, some with no symmetry and others with some rotational or reflective symmetry
- Split pins
- Sheets of paper larger than the stars
- Mirrors
- Paper and scissors for children to create their own stars

Preparation

- Fold some of the stars that have one line of symmetry in half.
- Fold some of the stars that have two lines of symmetry in half and then half again.
- Place some of the stars that have rotational symmetry onto the sheets of paper and attach them with a split pin through the centre of the star. Draw around the star so the outline can be seen on the paper.

What to do

- Let the children explore the stars you have prepared. What do they notice about the stars that have been folded? What happens when they rotate (turn) the stars around the split pin?
- Let the children explore the stars that were left unfolded and unpinned. Can they find the stars that are *symmetrical*? How many times can they fold them? How many times can they turn them before they get back to where the star started from? Can they find any stars that are *not symmetrical*?
- Can they make their own stars? Are they symmetrical? How are they symmetrical? Do they have *mirror symmetry* (they match when they are folded) or *rotational symmetry* (they sit in the shape when they are rotated about the centre)?

Young children have a natural propensity towards symmetry, particularly reflective symmetry in one vertical line. They also love using the word symmetrical!

Variations

- Children may also explore symmetry through making snowflakes by folding a circle of paper many times and cutting pieces out of it.
- You may go for a walk or look at photographs to see symmetry occurring naturally in many places, such as leaves, flowers and reflections in water.

How is this maths?

It is important for children to learn about symmetry because this will help them later to define shapes.

Day and night

Children can describe many differences between day and night.

Aims and objectives

- To talk about differences.
- To think about time (day/night).

Preparation

- Take the children outside.

What to do

- Talk about the sky they can see. What can they see today? Is it the same as yesterday? What might it be like tomorrow?
- What does the sky look like at night?
- Are there clouds at night? Talk about how clouds can't be seen because it is dark, but that the clouds are *in front* of the stars, or *closer* to us than the stars, so they hide the stars.
- Talk about the moon. What shapes can the moon be? Sometimes it is *circular* and other times it is a *crescent* shape.
- What do the children do during the day and during the night?

The moon can often be seen during the day – it is a misconception to think that the moon is only visible at night.

How is this maths?

The cycle of day and night is a repeating pattern observed in every 24 hours. It has a significant impact on the way humans lead their lives. Children find it easier to start thinking about one day as a unit of time than longer periods such as a week, month, year, etc. Thinking about how the shape of the moon changes over approximately one month also supports children in thinking about the passing of time and about pattern and shape.

Spacemen

Use the song to help children to think about taking away and counting backwards.

Aims and objectives

- To count backwards.
- To take away one.

Resources

- Cardboard flying saucer with five spacemen attached with a product such as Velcro or Blu-Tack®
- Or, rocket with five spacemen inside that can be removed

What to do

- Sing 'Five little men in a flying saucer'.
- As you reach the line in the song '... and one man flew away', stop singing and ask one child to remove one spaceman. Count together the remaining spacemen. Talk to the children about how 'there were five spacemen, one man flew away, so now there are four left' and so on. You also use the term *take away* as the spaceman is being removed from the spaceship.
- Sing the song again. Before counting the remaining spacemen, count backwards from five until you reach the number of spacemen who are in the spaceship. Check you are right by counting them forwards as well.
- Encourage the children to use their fingers to represent the spacemen. Start with five fingers, then put one finger down as the spaceman flies away or as you count backwards. 'How many fingers are left? Let's count the spacemen left.'

If you are not familiar with the tune, search YouTube for 'five little men in a flying saucer nationalelfservice' for a high-quality version of the song to use with the children.

Variation

Other songs provide opportunity for counting backwards and taking away. See pages 99–102 in the Songs and Chants chapter for more ideas.

How is this maths?

Children need to learn that *taking away* one is related to *counting backwards in ones*. They can also begin to develop their understanding of *subtraction as 'taking away'* using this type of activity. Using fingers to represent objects helps children to begin to abstract mathematical ideas – their fingers are an abstract representation of the spacemen. Later on they will understand that numbers themselves are abstract and can be used to represent counting (five spacemen, five blocks, five lots of ten, 5*x* and so on) and measurement (five o'clock, five years old, five metres, five degrees and so on).

Aliens

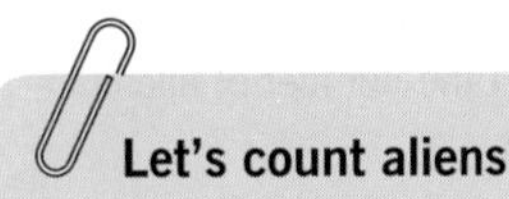

Let's count aliens!

Aims and objectives

- To count.
- To talk about pattern.

Resources

- Book: *Aliens Love Underpants* by Claire Freedman

Preparation

- Read *Aliens Love Underpants*.

What to do

- Discuss the patterns on the underpants inside the front cover. Which is their favourite pair of underpants? Why? What would they like to have on their own pair of underpants?
- Discuss the features of the aliens. How many legs do they have? Arms? Eyes? Antennae? Hair? And so on.
- How many aliens do they think are inside the underpants leg? How do they know? What do other children think? Discuss answers and praise any answers that have a logical reason given.

Encourage children to use their fingers to count the features on the aliens. This helps them with understanding that counting involves 1-to-1 correspondence (i.e. one number name to one item being counted).

How is this maths?

Children need to understand that anything can be counted. It is more difficult for children to count items that are not lined up. Being able to identify pattern is a fundamental aspect of mathematics. Working out the number of aliens in the underpants leg helps children to visualise quantity.

Design an alien

This activity provides lots of opportunity for you and the children to talk about number and to count.

Aims and objectives

- To count.
- To identify attributes.

Resources

- Book: *Aliens Love Underpants* by Claire Freedman
- Paper
- Paint, crayons, pencils or the media you wish the children to use

Preparation

- Read *Aliens Love Underpants* or another book that has pictures of aliens for the children to observe.

What to do

- Ask the children to imagine an alien themselves. Can they tell you how many legs it has? How many arms? Eyes? Teeth? Hairs? What is special about their alien?
- Encourage the children to paint, draw or construct their alien. Throughout this time, talk to the children about the number of features they are putting on the alien. Encourage them to count the features.
- Ask questions such as 'How many more arms do you need to draw?', or make observations such as 'I see you have drawn four eyes on the left and four eyes on the right. There are the same number of eyes on each side'.

Variation

Dress up like aliens! Discuss how many legs, arms, eyes etc the aliens have. How do they move? Where do they sleep? Act out being an alien. Talk about how having more arms might assist in certain jobs, or having more eyes might help them to see more things at the same time.

How is this maths?

This activity encourages children to talk about number and to practise counting and adding (by counting on).

Chapter 4
Fishing

Introduction

If you are planning to turn your classroom into an underwater environment try attaching light-blue cellophane and fish the children have made to the windows and hanging other underwater sea creatures from the ceiling. Strips of blue, green and clear cellophane interspersed between the creatures adds a watery feel also.

I've caught a big one!

Children practise their physical skills to catch the 'big one'!

Aims and objectives

- To identify numbers.
- To make numbers beyond 9.

Resources

- Laminated numbers 0–9 that are coloured to look like fish, with a paper clip attached
- 'Fishing rods': sticks that have a string hanging from the top, with a magnet at the end

Preparation

- Set up a 'pond' with the laminated numbers displayed in it.

What to do

- Children 'fish' for numbers of their choice, or fish for any number.
- Talk about the number that they have caught. What is that number? Can you count up to that number? Do you know a number that is smaller than that number? A number that is bigger?
- When all the fish have been caught, can they order them from lowest to highest number?
- Encourage the children to place two of the numbers (as digits) together to become another number. Can they name the number? What about three digits?

Tips

- **When the 'fish' are placed together, they become *digits*, rather than *numbers*. So, for example, '6' is a one-digit number when it is on its own. However, when in '36', '6' becomes a digit in a two-digit number. It is important to distinguish between 'number' and 'digit' to avoid confusion later on.**
- **You may wish to vary the size of the numbers, for example make a large '2' but a smaller '7'. This could lead to discussion about the order of numbers and how that differs from their physical size!**

Variations

Blindfold one fisherman. The other children offer clues for the fisherman to identify the fish that has been caught. E.g. 'It is an even number. It is a number greater than 6. Half of the number is 4'.

How is this maths?

Understanding the importance of ordering numbers correctly helps children to become confident counters and, later, use this skill to add, subtract, multiply and divide. Understanding how digits are used to represent numbers supports children's understanding of place value. Offering opportunities for children to talk about the properties of numbers in an open-ended way helps them to develop their understanding of number.

Go Fish!

This is a variation on the traditional card game as the children move with the cards.

Aims and objectives

- To familiarise the children with numbers.
- To learn problem solving and logical thinking.

Resources

- White A5 cards with sets of coloured numbers, laminated. The number of cards used will depend on the size of the group playing the game. For 28 children you may wish to use:

BLUE	YELLOW	RED	GREEN
10	10	10	10
11	11	11	11
12	12	12	12
13	13	13	13
14	14	14	14
15	15	15	15
16	16	16	16

Preparation

- Ensure there is a large space to play this game
- It may be helpful to draw a line in the centre of the space to keep the two groups apart

What to do

- Hand out the cards, one to each child.
- Choose seven children to stand in one group and then another seven children to stand in a second group facing them.

- The remainder of the class sit along the side, watching and keeping their cards hidden.
- The children in the two groups talk within each group and decide if they have any sets or groups of the same number. Encourage the children to stand together if they have a partner.
- Ask the first group to identify a number that they would like, that will help them make a set of four numbers the same. They ask the other group if they have that number. If the other group does, the child(ren) holding the card(s) move(s) to sit with group one and specifically with the other children holding that number. If the other group does not, all the children in the group shout out 'Go Fish!' and the group must choose one child from the side to join them.
- The groups take turns to ask for numbers. When a group of four numbers has been gathered, those four children sit at the back of their group to watch.
- The winning side is the group with the most children sitting at the back (i.e. the highest number of sets gathered).

Tips

- **You can substitute the numbers for any where the children require reinforcement or practice.**
- **Encourage the children to persuade their peers as to which number to ask for, and to explain their thinking to them.**

Variations

- You may wish to reduce the number of cards in a set to three, instead of four. This may speed the game up but will reduce the amount of opportunity for discussion.
- Instead of sitting at the back of the group the children can hand in their cards to the teacher and receive a new card, sitting at the side to join in again.
- Instead of being chosen, children can line up at the side and join a group in turn.

How is this maths?

This strategic game helps to develop children's logical thinking. The children need to use mathematical talk to identify the number that they want to ask for.

Fish race

Who will come first, second or third in this race with their fish?

Aims and objectives

- To use ordinal language (first, second, third and so on).
- To understand speed.
- To understand distance.

Resources

- Simple paper cut-outs of fish (cut from A4 size), one per child
- Sheets of newspaper, approximately 8–10

Preparation

- The children may want to colour their own fish, or write their name on them to help them to identify their own fish during the races.
- Fold each of the double-spread newspaper sheets several times so that it is about the size of an A4 sheet of paper. The number you will require will depend on how many children are competing at the same time.
- This is best carried out in a large space.

What to do

- Line up a small group of children behind the starting line with their fish.
- On 'go', the children move the newspaper up and down quickly to create a draught behind their own fish, so that the fish moves with the wind along the floor.
- The children continue to move their fish along until all the children have crossed the finish line.
- Repeat the steps above with the remaining children until everyone has had a go.

- You may hold semi-finals and finals with those children who crossed the finish line in their heat first, second or third.
- Pass out gold, silver and bronze medals for the three top competitors. You may want to display the winners, with photographs of the children holding their fish.

Tip **Give the children time to practise moving their fish.**

Variation

Some children may like to experiment with fish that are different sizes or made from different materials. Which do they think is most effective?

How is this maths?

The children use ordinal language to discuss who came first, second and third. Solving problems such as 'which is the most effective way to move the newspaper?' or 'which is the fastest fish design?' helps children to consider cause and effect.

Five little fish

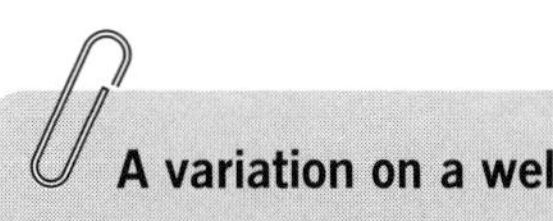

A variation on a well-known song.

Aims and objectives

- To count backwards.
- To learn about taking away.
- To learn the days of the week.

Resources

- Lyrics (see below)
- Fish costumes or puppets
- Days of the week and numbers 1–5 displayed on cards to hold

Preparation

- Children can dress up or put on fish puppets.

What to do

- Sing the song together (lyrics below).
  Lyrics:
  (Tune: 'Five little ducks')

  Five little fish went swimming on Monday
  Through the water and far far away
  Mother Fish called, 'It's time to come back'
  But only four little fish swam back

  Four little fish went swimming on Tuesday . . .
  Three little fish went swimming on Wednesday . . .
  Two little fish went swimming on Thursday . . .
  One little fish went swimming on Friday . . . but no little fish came swimming back

(Slowly)
Sad Mother Fish went swimming on Saturday
Through the water and far far away
Mother Fish cried, 'Please don't stay away'
And five little fish came back on Sunday!
(Cheer)

- Between verses, talk about how many fish stayed away. Model sentences such as, 'There were five fish and then one stayed away, so there were four that came back'. Show how five fish with one moving away leaves four.
- Between verses, discuss what the next day of the week will be.

Variations

- The children can have fish finger puppets, or show the number of fingers representing the number of fish.
- Start with ten fish, and sing the song with less discussion about the next number.

How is this maths?

Counting backwards and thinking about 'taking away' are two early ways to think about subtraction. When showing a representation, such as a fish puppet, the children are linking number to the number of objects represented. When they are using their fingers they are using abstract representation of the numbers. Knowing the names of the days of the week and that they repeat in a particular order is important for children to think about pattern and how we record time and dates.

Nothing but net

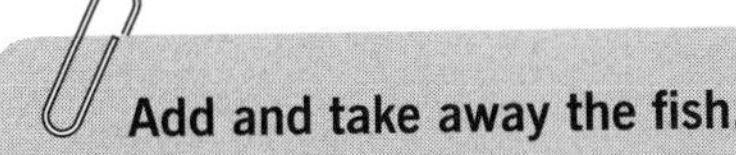

Add and take away the fish.

Aims and objectives

- To learn how to count on.
- To take away.

Resources

- Small toy fish or small cardboard fish that have been cut out and laminated for durability
- One 'net' per child (optional and may not be desirable for some children, see tip below)
- Bag with small cards, as listed below

Yellow cards:

Catch 1 fish	Catch 1 fish	Catch 1 fish	Catch 1 fish
Catch 2 fish	Catch 2 fish	Catch 2 fish	Catch 2 fish
Catch 3 fish	Catch 3 fish	Catch 3 fish	Catch 3 fish

Red cards:

Throw back 1 fish	Throw back 1 fish	Throw back 1 fish	Throw back 1 fish
Throw back 2 fish	Throw back 2 fish	Throw back 2 fish	Throw back 2 fish
Throw back 3 fish	Throw back 3 fish	Throw back 3 fish	Throw back 3 fish

Preparation

- Place the fish in a 'fish tank' or in the 'sea' (a central place on floor or table where all the children can reach).
- If you wish to use nets, provide each child with a fishing net.

What to do

- Children take turns to draw a card from the bag. They follow the instructions on the card by gathering fish from the central pot, or returning them. They then return the card to the bag.
- The winner is the first child to get to a nominated number of fish (for example 15 or 20 fish).
- If a red card is drawn and the child does not have that number of fish to return, they either miss a turn, or draw further cards until they can follow the action.

Tip **Children who require more counting practice may find it easier to have their fish lined up in front of them rather than in a net.**

Variations

- Use larger numbers and increase the number of fish that have to be caught.
- You may have only the yellow cards in the bag, for counting on only. Alternatively each child may start with 20 fish and the winner is the child who has the most remaining after one child's net is empty.

How is this maths?

This game of chance gives children the opportunity to count and look at the effect on their total number of fish of 'catching' (adding) or 'throwing back' (subtracting) individual fish.

Rainbow fish

Aims and objectives

- To recognise numerals.
- To learn accurate counting.

Resources

- Book: *The Rainbow Fish* by Marcus Pfister
- Fish templates (see illustration) – one per child
- Counters
- Dice

Preparation

- Read *The Rainbow Fish* to the children.
- Provide each child with a 'Rainbow Fish' template.
- Children cover their template with counters on the scales.

What to do

- Children take turns to roll the dice and remove the number of scales (counters) that the dice shows.
- Children must roll the correct number to finish.
- The winner is the child who has managed to give away all their scales first.

When talking with the children about the 'Rainbow Fish' giving away his scales, discuss what happens to the remaining number of scales on his body (they reduce in number).

Variation

Children may share one template between one pair of children, for the children to count together and help each other play the game.

How is this maths?

When children use dice they see an abstract representation of a particular number. With experience children will develop knowledge about what each representation means without having to count the number of dots.

Chapter 5
Games

Introduction

You are likely to have an area in your classroom where games are kept. Are they accessible to all the children all of the time? Or do you bring games out for the children to play with at different times? Perhaps you use a combination of these. Of course games can be played as they are traditionally designed. However, you may want to think about the extent to which you could adapt the games to a larger or smaller scale. For example, the children could help their toys to play hopscotch on a table, or a giant snakes and ladders board could be drawn with chalk in the outdoor area. Dice also come in a range of sizes.

Games with dice

Children learn another way to represent number through using dice.

Counting on and back

Use the dice to see how many squares to count on or back.

Aims and objectives

- To take turns.
- To practise counting.

Resources

- Dice
- A 'board', either indoors or out

Preparation

- If necessary create an outdoor game 'board' to reflect the theme.

What to do

- Children take turns throwing the dice and moving their counter along the requisite number of squares.

Ensure the children learn that they start counting on the *next* square and not the one their counter is already resting on. This helps them when they are 'counting on' in addition.

Variations

If playing on a larger scale, the children could be the 'counters' and move themselves along the board. To practise subtraction use two dice and move along the difference of the two numbers on the dice. Alternatively use one regular dice and another that shows '–' and '+' or the terms '*take*' and '*add*', or '*forward*' and '*back*'.

How is this maths?

Children practise counting on board games. Using the dice provides an opportunity for the children to see that numbers can be represented in different ways. Counting on or counting back along the board is a useful context for the children to learn about early addition and subtraction.

Snakes and ladders

An alternative three-dimensional construction approach to this traditional board game.

Aims and objectives

- To practise counting.
- To understand greater than/less than.
- To practise problem-solving.

Resources

- Fabric cut into strips to represent the snakes
- Cardboard or paper cut into ladders
- Large number square, say 1–50
- One blank dice (prepared as below)
- One regular dice
- Counters, one per child
- One set of smaller number cards with the same numbers as are on the board, say 1–50

Preparation

- Lay out the number square.
- On one blank dice draw a ladder and a snake on the same face. Leave the remaining five faces blank.

What to do

- The children start to play the board by rolling the two dice.
- If the 'blank' dice rolls a plain face the child moves their counter along the board as they normally would, according to the number on the regular dice.
- If they roll the face that shows a snake/ladder then they take a number card from the pile.
- If the number is *greater than* the square they are currently on, they place a ladder from their current square to the square on the number card. If it is *less than* their occupied square, they place a snake between the two squares.
- The child moves along the ladder/snake in the same turn.
- The next child takes their turn to roll the two dice and the game continues.

Have a length of fabric for making the snakes and allow the children to cut the fabric to the desired length. Encourage the children to think about how the snakes' curves have an impact on the *length* of the fabric required. When the board is complete photograph it, print out the photo onto an A4 page and laminate it. This will build up a stock of board games the children can play in class or during rainy lunch times.

Variations

Constructing this game can be applied to a range of contexts, such as 'Jack and the Beanstalk' (where the ladders become beanstalks and the snakes become giants' boots or an axe), 'The Grand old Duke of York' (where different shades of green fabric are used for going up and down hills) or weather (using sunbeams for ladders and streams of raindrops for snakes).

How is this maths?

The children are *counting*, *matching*, *recognising* and *reading* numbers. They are also *problem-solving* and using *reasoning* as they talk about the development of the board.

Floor robot games[1]

Floor robots, such as Bee-bot, Roamer or Pixie, are fun and easy for children to use.

Floor robot competition

Whose robot will win the game?

Aims and objectives

- To learn about addition using counting on.
- To learn about subtraction using counting back.

Resources

- One or two floor robots
- Two sets of number cards that are the same length as the robot moving one step
- Two dice, one red and one blue

Preparation

- Set out the number cards in two lines with a little space between the two lines.

Robot	1	2	3	4	5	6	7	8	9	10
Robot	1	2	3	4	5	6	7	8	9	10

[1] Floor robots can be purchased from the following places (amongst others): Bee-bot (TTS online. Visit www.tts-group.co.uk/shops/tts/Products/PD1723538/Bee-Bot-Floor-Robot/); Roamer (Valiant Technologies. Visit www.valiant-technology.com/uk/pages/standard_roamers.php); Pixie and Pippin (Swallow Systems. Visit www.swallow.co.uk).

What to do

- Divide the children into two teams.
- Place one floor robot next to, but not on, each of the number 1s on the number track.
- The teams take turns to roll the two dice. The red dice shows how many squares the robot can move *forward* (program the robot to take these steps) and the blue dice shows how many squares the robot should move *backward* (then program the robot to take these steps back).
- The winning team is the team who makes the target first.

The game may take some time to play. To speed things up, put larger numbers on the red dice. Once the children have become adept at setting the robot to go forward for the red number and back for the blue, encourage them to visualise the moves the robot would take then ask them how the robot could take the shortest route to that number.

Variation

To work with different numbers, use a different start and end number in the number track.

How is this maths?

The children are beginning to use the number track to look at *counting on* and *counting back*. The robot is moving in the same way that they will later use other *number tracks* and then *number lines* to carry out *addition* and *subtraction*.

Floor robot target

Children enjoy estimating and then getting the robot to hit the target.

Aims and objectives

- To estimate length.
- To create instructions.
- To check the reasonableness of estimations.

Resources

- Masking tape or similar
- Two floor robots

Preparation

- Mask out a target zone on the floor with the tape.
- Set the floor robots some distance from the target.

What to do

- Divide the children into two teams. Each will be responsible for one of the robots.
- Encourage the children to discuss in their teams how many robot body lengths the robots are away from the centre of the target.
- One representative from each team will program the robot with the estimated distance.
- The team who comes the closest to the bullseye wins.

Tip **You may put a skittle or similar in the centre for the robot to knock down. Talk about how much further the robot needed to travel, or the distance the robot travelled too far.**

Variations

- Different scores could be given for reaching different areas – the closer to the target, the higher the score.
- Face the robots away from the target so the children need to think about rotating the robot and using quarter turns and half turns as well as length.
- Instead of one target only, create a golf course around the floor within which the teams must program their robots to touch each target. The team with the lowest number of moves wins.

How is this maths?

Estimation is a key mathematical skill. By estimating the distance the robot needs to travel, the children are then able to check the reasonableness of their estimations and amend future estimations accordingly.

Beanbags

A resource that is easy to hold and throw.

Aims and objectives

- To visualise numbers.
- To understand addition as 'how many altogether'.
- To understand subtraction as 'how many more' or the 'difference'.

Resources

- Five small beanbags for throwing
- Bag or small container for holding the beanbags
- Bucket or bin or similar for throwing the beanbags into

Preparation

- None required.

What to do

- Show the children you have five beanbags and count them together.
- Throw some of the beanbags into the bucket. Ask the children, 'How many have I got left?' Check together by counting.
- Repeat, encouraging the children to throw the beanbags too.

Some beanbags may miss. Ask how many got into the bucket and how many missed. This is an opportunity to add together three numbers – the beanbags in the bucket, those on the floor and those yet to be thrown.

Variations

- Ask the children to close their eyes and listen to you or other children dropping the beanbags into the bucket. Repeat with different numbers of beanbags.
- Use other items that may be thrown or dropped into the target.
- Play simply to see how many beanbags can be thrown into the bucket: split the children into two groups where members take turns throwing the beanbags into the bucket. The first team to reach a pre-agreed score is the winning team.

How is this maths?

This is an opportunity for the children to think about the different ways the number 5 can be created, for example 1 and 4, 2 and 2 and 1, and so on. By *visualising* the beanbags in the bucket the children will be able to undertake these simple calculations more effectively.

Hide-and-count

This is similar to the traditional Kim's Game.

Aims and objectives

- To practise counting.
- To visualise a number.

Resources

- Any objects that can be handled, for counting
- A tea towel or similar for covering the objects or a bag/box for placing them into

Preparation

- None required,

What to do

- Count out three objects.
- Cover them.
- Show one being taken away.
- Ask, 'How many are still under the cover?'
- Reveal and check.
- Repeat with different numbers.

Tip

Start with smaller numbers and then increase the number of objects being used. When larger numbers are used, start by taking away small numbers or half of the whole set.

Variation

Children can play with each other.

How is this maths?

Children are counting and visualising number. They are thinking about subtraction as *taking away*.

Make a group

A fun way to burn off some energy or to make groups for physical development or PE activities.

Aims and objectives

- To practise counting.
- To understand problem solving.

Resources

- Large amounts of space

Preparation

- None required.

What to do

- Call out a number and ask the children to make groups consisting of that number of children.
- Any children who do not find themselves in a group can join in again for the next round.

Tip

This game helps encourage teamwork. The practitioner/teacher might time each attempt and encourage the children to improve (reduce) the length of time it takes them to get into their groups.

Variation

This can be played in a competitive way where any children who do not find themselves in a group can watch from the side while the next groups form, until there is one child left who is the winner.

How is this maths?

During the activity the children will practise counting. They will also be working out if their group is *too big* or *too small* – both key mathematical concepts.

On your bike!

Children enjoy riding their bikes, scooters or tricycles around a given route.

Aims and objectives

- To follow directions.
- To give directions.

Resources

- Tricycles or scooters or bicycles
- An area pre-painted or taped out with roads for the children to ride on
- Lollipop-type 'stop' and 'go' sign

Preparation

- The children may design and create the route with you.

What to do

- The children move around the route by foot or using the play transport.
- One child may be the lollipop holder, telling the travellers to *go* or *stop* along the route.
- Ask, 'Is there a T-junction? Which way are you going to go now?'

Tip **This activity offers you the opportunity to talk a lot to the children about staying on the *left* of the road and about going *through, over, under, between* and *zig-zagging* around objects on the route.**

Variation

Add traffic lights. 'What are the colours? What do the colours tell us to do?'

How is this maths?

There is a lot of mathematical vocabulary that can be used in this activity. Giving and following directions requires the children to use their reasoning skills.

Hide-and-seek

A fun way to give friends directions to a hidden object.

Aims and objectives

- To use positional language.
- To estimate distance.

Resources

- A set of small objects

Preparation

- Place a number of small objects around the room or outside, partially hidden from sight.

What to do

- Ask the children to look around the room or outdoor space to find the hidden objects. Explain they are not to give away the location of any objects they find.
- After a short time, bring the children together. Encourage the children to take turns to describe the location of one object for others to find without pointing!

Tip **The small objects can be related to the current theme or topic. Encourage the children to use positional language such as *on*, *under*, *next to*, *behind*, and so on.**

Variations

- One at a time (or in pairs) tell the children if they are warm, hot, cooler, etc. as they move around the space to identify the hidden location of an object.
- The child(ren) could leave the room while the remainder of the children hide an object and then give the directions themselves.

How is this maths?

The children are using positional language to describe the position of an object in their environment. This is very early geometry. If playing the variation above, the children are estimating distance from an object by using 'hot', 'warm', 'freezing', and so on. Using only words and no gestures is very difficult.

Hopscotch

A variation on the traditional game, which children can play independently or in a small group.

Aims and objectives

- To recognise numbers.
- To practise counting.

Resources

- A hopscotch area painted or drawn outdoors, or taped on the floor indoors
- A small object to throw, such as a beanbag or small toy

Preparation

- Tape the hopscotch outline on the carpet or hall floor if no room outdoors.

What to do

- Children throw the beanbag onto the hopscotch area.
- They hop or jump on the numbers of the hopscotch, avoiding the number the beanbag landed on.

Tips

- **Talk about what number they have missed out (because the beanbag is on it). Discuss the two numbers it is between. Ask, 'What number is it after? What number is it before?'**
- **Talk about hopping and jumping and the difference: one leg/two legs.**

Variation

Play in the more traditional way, by throwing the beanbag onto the numbers in succession and allowing the next person to have their turn if the bag does not land in the correct square.

How is this maths?

By playing hopscotch the children are recognising numbers and counting.

Chapter 6
All about me

Introduction

Children love to talk about themselves and explore their own bodies. This chapter contains a wide range of activities that explore a variety of mathematical concepts. Take and display photographs of the children undertaking the activities. Displaying these with labels that discuss the mathematical skills that were used (for example, counting: 'I have ten toes,' says Ishmal) will support children beyond the activities themselves.

My body

We can explore our bodies using lots of mathematical ideas.

Aims and objectives

- To practise counting.
- To learn about estimating.

Resources

- None required.

Preparation

- None required.

What to do

- This is an activity based on discussion. Ask the following sorts of questions:
- 'What can you find that there are then of?' (Fingers, toes.)
- 'What can you find that there are two of?' (Legs, arms, eyes, ears, feet, hands, eyebrows, nostrils, knees, ankles, armpits.) 'Why are there two?' (Talk about the *symmetry* of their bodies.)
- 'What can you find that there is one of?' (Nose, belly button.) 'Why is there one?' (Talk about the *midline* or *line of symmetry* of their bodies.)
- Count: 'How many teeth do you have? Do we all have the same number of teeth? Why/why not? How old are you?'
- Estimate: 'How many hairs do you think you might have?'

Tips

- **Draw around the children and make a template so they can identify the body parts.**
- **Although the last point above is an *estimation* activity, for your information there are, on average, 100,000 hairs on a human head, although this varies between individuals as well as according to the colour of a person's hair!**

Variations

Don't just stop at counting discrete numbers. Look at other ways to use numbers, e.g. continuous measures such as children's heights. Children can order themselves according to their height, or compare their height with those of toys or other objects in the room. They can also look at foot length or hand span, waist circumference and so on.

How is this maths?

Young children do not need to count two objects. They can look at a set of two and just know that there are two objects. This is because they develop the notion of 'twoness' very early. Thinking about larger numbers requires them to count. Estimating the number of hairs on their head will elicit a number of weird and wonderful numbers but this will excite them as they talk about all the really large numbers they know. Children are also thinking about symmetry, another intuitive concept. Finally, they are using comparing skills.

Travelling

Explore the different modes of transport that the children use and think about their various purposes.

Aims and objectives

- To represent data in a pictogram.
- To interpret data in a pictogram.

Resources

- Objects or pictures to represent different modes of transport

Preparation

- None required.

What to do

- Discuss, 'How do you normally travel to nursery/school?'
- Give each child an object or picture of their mode of transport
- Ask the children, 'How do we know *how many* people travel by car?' Talk about how having everyone sitting on the carpet all mixed up makes answering this question difficult. Ask for ideas about how it could be made easier. Steer the children into thinking about *grouping* themselves, still holding their objects/pictures.
- Ask the children 'Which is the *most popular* way to travel to nursery/school?' or '*How many more* people travel by car than walk?' Again talk about how this is a difficult problem to solve when the children are standing in groups. Steer the children into standing in rows so they can see which is the longest line.
- Line up the objects, or stick the pictures onto the wall.

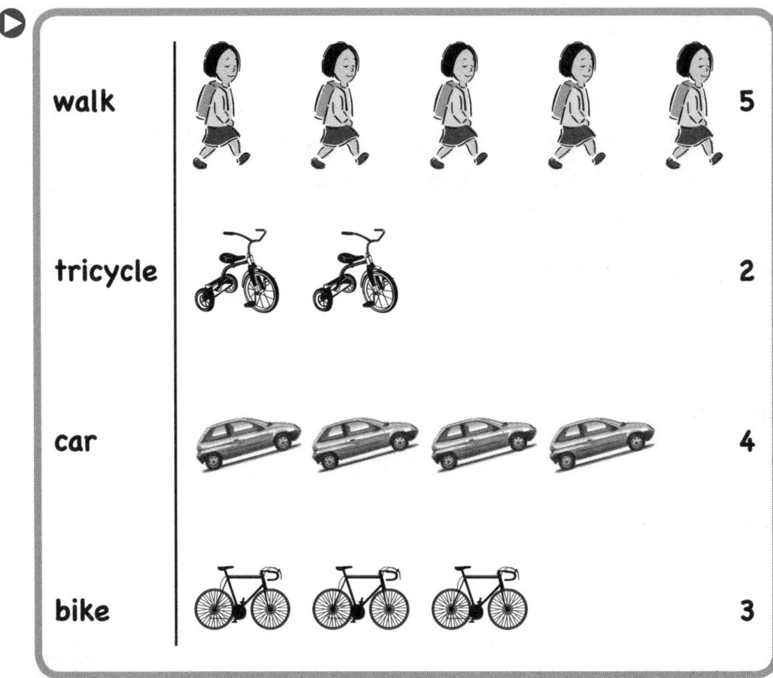

Tips

- Have a set of objects/pictures ready that are not going to be used, for example an aeroplane. Talk about why there are no children using this mode of transport.
- With higher-attaining children 'trick' them by spacing out one of the smaller sets of pictures on the wall, and state that more children used that mode of transport. Talk about why your statement is incorrect, and encourage the children to rectify the error. Discuss why it is important to have the same size pictures/objects and to ensure even spaces between them.

Variations

- This can be used with any topic about ourselves, such as types of shoes being worn, shoe size, birthday months, eye colour, number of siblings, favourite books and so on.

- If introducing block graphs, instead of giving the children an object or picture of the mode of transport give them a particular colour of a Unifix® or Multilink® block, for example, so they can make a tower to answer the questions. Similarly provide each child with a coloured square card to stick onto the wall.

How is this maths?

This approach to data handling helps children to make links between graphs and real data items. It helps them to understand that representing data in graphical form can help them to make more sense of it. Having items that are going to be the *null set* (such as aeroplanes in this example) provides an opportunity for children to understand how the *empty set* can also be represented on a graph.

My day

This gives children an opportunity to think about their daily routines in chronological order.

Aims and objectives

- To order events.
- To use time-related vocabulary.

Resources

- Pictures of routines that children would undertake during the day (e.g. getting up, brushing teeth, breakfast, lunch, tea, having a bath, feeding pets, going to bed, travelling to/from nursery/school, going to the mosque, visiting grandparents, playing)
- Blank cards for children to draw their own routines that may not already be represented
- Glue if the children are going to stick the pictures in order

Preparation

- Laminate the pictures if you wish to use them again.

What to do

- Talk with the children about what they do during one day.
- Provide them with the pictures of the events they talk about, in any order.
- Ask the children to order the pictures. Ask questions such as, 'What do you do *first* in the *morning*?', 'What happens *next*?', 'What is the very *last* thing you do at *night*?', and 'Is there anything that happens *between* these two?'
- Encourage the children to tell the story of their day, using as many time-related words as possible. Include times of the day such as morning, afternoon, evening, night, noon, dawn, dusk, day and night.

Have more than one card to allow for repeats during the day, and be prepared for surprises as not all children do what you think they would do in the order you might expect!

Variation

Use *times* and match events with *analogue clocks*. For example, lunch might be at 12 o'clock and bedtime might be at 7 o'clock.

How is this maths?

Understanding the order of events and what time they happen helps children to *sequence*. Sequencing is an important skill to use when attempting to solve problems.

Chapter 7
Houses and homes

Introduction

Many of the activities in this chapter can be undertaken both indoors and out. To support the activities you could set up an estate agents in the role-play area or go for a walk to explore the different types of houses nearby. Making dens and model houses can be carried out on a very large or a smaller scale, and they can be made out of a wide range of materials.

Other people's homes

Children find it fascinating to learn about the way other people's homes are constructed.

Aims and objectives

- To talk about shape.

Resources

- Pictures of non-traditional-British homes (e.g. igloo, tepee, mud homes, homes on stilts, tree houses, houseboats)

Preparation

- None required.

What to do

- Discuss what the houses in the surrounding area look like and how they are built. Talk about the *rectangular* doors, windows and walls. Discuss the construction, such as the *triangular* roof, and what materials have been used in the building, such as *rectangular prism* bricks.
- Explain to the children that you are going to show them some pictures of other types of houses. Do they know any? Encourage them to discuss what they already know about other types of houses.
- Show the children the pictures. Discuss how they are built to keep them stable. Identify the shapes within the dwellings.

Tips

- **Adapt the first point (above) as appropriate to your immediate area.**
- **Model appropriate two- and three-dimensional shape language. For example, a roof may be *triangular*, not a *triangle*. Most children are able very quickly to use appropriate language when it has been modelled by an adult through careful discussion.**
- **Explore why particular shapes are used in different constructions. For example, igloos are dome-shaped because an arch is a strong shape. The dome also requires no other structure (such as beams or poles) to keep it up. Additionally, a dome has the smallest possible surface area, which provides the best insulation.**

Variation

Ask the children to design and model their own house. Discuss where it is going to be located, what materials are going to be used and what shapes it needs to use in order to make it fit for purpose.

How is this maths?

In this activity the children are exploring how shapes are used in construction in order to make the construction strong and fit for purpose.

A nonsense house

Get creative with this nonsense design activity.

Aims and objectives

- To use shape-related language.
- To think about the properties of shapes.

Resources

- Selection of coloured paper shapes
- A4 paper
- Glue

Preparation

- You may wish to make your own nonsense house to show the children.

What to do

- Talk to the children about their houses and why certain features are the shape they are (e.g. 'Why is a door *rectangular*?'). Include items in the house in the discussion (e.g. 'Why is the table *flat*?').
- Now encourage the children to imagine a nonsense world where there were houses that could not be used. For example, a *spherical* house that sat wobbling on top of a hill, a *square-based pyramid* for a bed that was very uncomfortable or a scooter that had *triangular prisms* for wheels.
- Give the children an everyday object, or ask them to think of one of their own. (For example, a car, a house, a bicycle, a table, a television, a sofa).
- Encourage the children to talk with a friend about their object. How could they make it as nonsensical as possible? Then share the answers with the group.
- Arrange the shapes of the object onto an A4 sheet and, when ready, glue them down.
- Share again once finished.

Tips

- **Ensure the children continue to talk about the shapes. They may need to talk about the materials being used, but the focus of this activity is the shapes being used.**
- **You may put the designs together and jointly write a story about a day in the life of Mr and Mrs Shape who live in Nonsenseland.**

Variation

Using junk modelling instead of paper shapes to make the nonsense items.

How is this maths?

The children are using their knowledge of the properties of shapes to create objects that are complete nonsense. By producing a design of something that would not be fit for purpose they are thinking in a creative way about the properties of shapes and why we use specific shapes for particular functions.

Making dens

Children love to make a den and entertain friends and adults in it!

Aims and objectives

- To practise problem solving
- To learn about measurement

Resources

- Items for making a den, inside or out
- Cups, fruit or biscuits and water (or role-play tea-making items)

Preparation

- Check there is an appropriate space for this activity, inside or out.

What to do

- Either independently or with support the children can make a den, choosing from a selection of available resources.
- Once constructed, give the children afternoon tea or a snack and eat it with them in the den. Encourage them to pour the water and share the food out evenly.

During the construction, talk with the children about their design and why they are choosing to construct it that way. Help them to make sense of the space they are using and model appropriate propositional language, such as *under*, *next to*, *over* and *between*, as well as early geometrical language such as *cover*, *big*, *corner*, *top* and *side*. When pouring the water talk about *nearly full*, *full*, *empty*, *half-full* and *half-empty*.

Variation

Have afternoon tea in a pre-existing place, such as a Wendy house or outside on the field.

How is this maths?

While the children are creating their den they are solving problems related to the construction. For example they need to reason about the best materials to use and they are communicating mathematically with each other. Pouring water into cups offers an opportunity to develop concepts related to *capacity*. *Sharing* food leads to *division by grouping* later on.

That's just up our street!

Ordering the houses along a street provides a good opportunity for a lot of mathematical talk about numbers.

Aims and objectives

- To recognise numbers.
- To learn about number patterns.

Resources

- Photographs or drawings of front doors with the house number clearly labelled
- A large street or map drawn out where the houses can be placed (optional)

Preparation

- If using a street to lay the houses upon ensure this is out before the children start the activity. Make sure it is securely fastened because the children will bump it as they position the houses in the correct places.

What to do

- Look at the photos or the pictures of the houses. What can we see on them? (The house numbers.)
- Ask, 'Can you work out who might be neighbours? How do you know that those two houses are neighbouring?'
- Encourage the children to place the houses in the correct order, along both sides of the street.

Tips

- **This can be used as part of a theme or topic on the postman and mail. The children could become the post office staff, sorting the mail and then delivering the post to the houses along the street in the most efficient manner.**
- **Encourage the children to look at the starting number and identify any patterns they see along the road (for example one side will have house numbers that end in 2, 4, 6, 8 and 0 only). Talk about the *odd* and *even* numbers.**

Variations

- Some cul-de-sacs contain houses that are in *numerical order*. Younger children or lower-attaining children could be encouraged to place houses around a cul-de-sac that comes off a larger road.
- You may provide a range of properties to challenge further the children's understanding of number. For example, there may be a factory or warehouse that is numbered 24–28 because it takes up three plots on one side of the road.

How is this maths?

This activity encourages the children to look at *patterns*. One pattern uses *counting numbers*, where they cross the street each time they get to the next number. Another pattern is to look at the *odd* and *even* numbers on each side of the street. Being able to spot patterns sets the foundation for later mathematical problems using more complex number patterns. This activity also helps them to see how numbers have a purpose (identifying a home) and how they give order and structure, which makes finding a particular home easier for any visitors.

My home

An opportunity for children to think about their own home a little more.

Aims and objectives

- To recognise and order numbers.
- To practise reasoning.

Resources

- None required

Preparation

- Encourage the children's families to talk with them about their own house number and the house numbers of friends, neighbours and family in preparation for this activity.

What to do

- Ask, 'What number house do you live at?', 'Who lives next to you?' and 'What number do they live at?'
- Ask, 'What rooms do you use in your house?', 'What times of the day do you use them?', 'Where would you go if you were hungry?', 'Where would you sit to eat?' and 'Where do you go when you are getting tired?'

Some children may not know their own house number. You may wish to look up the children's records before this activity to help them complete it. It is likely that many of the children will not know their neighbours' house numbers. They may be surprised to find that it is not a number immediately before or after their own house number!

Variation

Talk further about the numbers that the children live at. What might '23a' mean? What about 1/33 in a row of flats? Does anyone not have a number? Perhaps they have a name, like 'Rose Cottage', to identify their house.

How is this maths?

In this activity children are talking about numbers in an everyday context that is familiar to them. They are also able to talk about the purpose that certain rooms have in their home and reason why this might be the case.

We've got it covered!

A chance to look at repeating patterns on the walls in our homes.

Aims and objectives

- To identify repeating patterns.

Resources

- Wallpaper samples
- Wallpaper border samples

Preparation

- You may wish to make a *unit block* of each wallpaper or border sample by identifying which is the *repeating unit*, cutting it out and mounting it on cardboard (or laminating it) so the children can move it around the larger section of wallpaper.

What to do

- Talk about how people decorate the walls of their homes. Some children will have painted surfaces, others will have tiles (particularly in the bathroom) and some will have wallpaper.
- Show one of the wallpapers or borders you have collected. Ask the children to describe what they can see. Encourage them to identify that the paper is made of repeating patterns.
- Can the children see how the pattern has been made to repeat? Has it been *slid* along the paper (*translated*), has it been *turned* (*rotated*) and/or has it been *flipped* (*reflected*)? If you have made a unit block from the sample use it to help the children describe what they can see.
- Divide the children into pairs or small groups, provide them with other samples and encourage them to work out how they are made.

Wallpaper and border samples can be gathered from decorating stores free of charge. Use wallpapers that the children will find attractive. Papers that use geometric figures enable children to use their mathematical language more than those with figures of popular cartoon characters.

Variation

When looking at celebrations or giving presents as a topic, use selections of gift-wrap instead of wallpaper.

How is this maths?

The children are exploring geometric patterns using early language related to transformational geometry. They will also begin to understand that patterns have no end and that they keep repeating.

Be an interior designer!

This is an enjoyable follow-up activity.

Aims and objectives

- To copy and continue a repeating pattern.
- To create a repeating pattern.

Resources

- Strips of paper approximately 10cm x 50cm
- Sponges or potatoes with shapes cut into them for printing
- Paint (limit to three colours)
- Mini white boards and markers, or scrap paper with crayons

Preparation

- Carry out the activity 'We've got it covered!' in preparation for this activity.

What to do

- Show the children a wallpaper border. Discuss the repeating pattern.
- Explain that the children (in pairs if you prefer) are going to design their own pattern.
- Show them the sponges/potatoes and discuss the shapes that are available to use.
- Reveal the paint colours they are able to use.
- Encourage them to talk with a partner about what shapes (limit this to two or three depending on their attainment) and what colour paint they will use.
- Ask the children to record their ideas on their mini whiteboards or scrap paper.
- The children will share with the group how their pattern repeats, both in terms of the shapes used and the colours used. If the children have rotated their shapes, discuss this also.
- Once the pattern designs have been finalised provide the large strips of paper, the sponges and paint for the children to create their own border.
- When finished, ask the children questions such as: 'What shape is the third shape?' 'When does that appear again?' 'And again?' 'What would the 15th shape be?' (ensure you select an ordinal number that is not on the pattern, so the children are required to visualise the continuing pattern); 'What shape is after/before the red square?' 'What is the next shape in your pattern?' 'How do you know the next shape is going to be yellow?' 'What is the basic unit you have used in your pattern?'

Tips

- **Throughout the printing process talk with the children about the shapes they are using and how the pattern *repeats*.**
- **Display the borders with typed-up explanations from the children about how they made their repeating pattern.**
- **You may show the children a television clip from an interior design programme that uses a wallpaper border.**
- **For younger children simply start a pattern for them and ask them to continue it. Limit the number of shapes to two or three and the number of colours to one or two.**

Variation

The children might print their own paper for covering a special book, t-shirt or ribbon, etc.

How is this maths?

The children have designed and made their own repeating geometric patterns. By asking them what comes next they are able to discuss the pattern. When explaining where the triangles appear they are linking the pattern to ordinal numbers (for example second, fourth, sixth and so on). Additionally they are *visualising* the pattern beyond what they can see on their border.

The doll's house

Small-world play always captures children's imaginations.

Aims and objectives

- To use propositional language.
- To learn how to order events.

Resources

- Doll's house with associated items

Preparation

- None required.

What to do

While a group of children are playing with the doll's house encourage them to talk about:

- What the dolls are doing. For example, going *up* the stairs, getting *in* bed.
- The day the dolls are having. 'What have the dolls been doing today?' Can the children place the events in order?
- Why the dolls are in a particular room. Ask, 'Is it lunchtime for the dolls? How are they going to get ready for lunch?' 'Can you help the dolls to get ready for bed?'

This structured play activity involves you modelling appropriate vocabulary and prompting the children to explore other mathematical ideas as the opportunity arises.

Variation

Using a farm, superhero's lair or other small-world area the same mathematical ideas can be explored in a context that might be more attractive to some children.

How is this maths?

Through small-world play children re-enact events that are real or imagined. It is possible for you to model and encourage children to use mathematical vocabulary through this natural behaviour. In this activity using positional language develops into geometric concepts, ordering events considers time-related concepts and associating tasks with rooms supports children's problem-solving and reasoning skills.

Chapter 8
The Teddy Bears' Picnic

Introduction

Planning and undertaking a teddy bears' picnic gives children an opportunity to collaborate on a project together. You may want to select one group of older children in the nursery to plan and run the picnic for all the children, or you could have the whole class arranging a day that involves friends and family as well. Running a few stalls or charging a small price for the food could also turn these activities into a fun fundraising event.

Choosing a picnic blanket

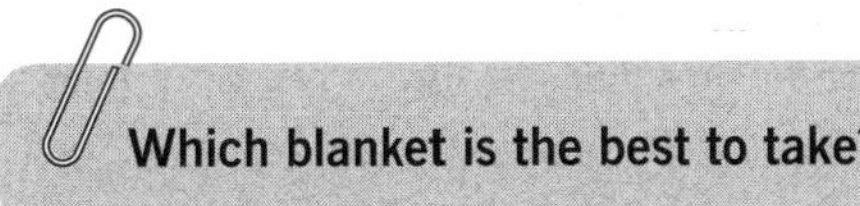

Aims and objectives

- To practise problem solving.
- To learn about area.

Resources

- A variety of different-sized blankets: some very small and, if possible, one or two that are too large

Preparation

- Jumble up the blankets and put them into a large box.

What to do

- Explain to the children that a picnic blanket is an essential item to take because it provides somewhere to sit and eat the picnic.
- Show the children the box and explain that no one can carry the whole box to the picnic, and that there are probably too many blankets in the box anyway.
- Ask the children if they would like to help prepare for the picnic by selecting the most appropriate blankets.
- Depending on the children either provide further support so they can identify a list of criteria for selecting blankets, or let the children explore the contents of the box and identify their own criteria through blanket selection.
- When complete, ask the children to explain why they chose the blankets they did.

Tips

- **Encourage the children to think about the number of children who can sit on each blanket. Talk about how many bottoms can fit on the blanket and how some blankets (for example those that are very long but skinny) might fit fewer bottoms than one that at first looks smaller.**
- **Be open-minded about the reasons for the children's selections. While you may want to talk about practicality, some children may feel that aesthetic reasons are more important!**

Variation

Any theme that requires the children to consider an area of a shape could involve some sorting. For example, the children may need to decide which tables to use for a Red Nose Day table-top sale at lunch time, or which wrapping paper to use to wrap the differently sized boxes.

How is this maths?

Exploring area in this way helps children to think about *conservation of area*. Understanding that the area of a shape may be different to the visual signals the shape gives to the brain is a notion that children will understand with a lot of practical experience.

Time for the picnic?

Thinking about what time the picnic will be held helps children to use vocabulary related to telling the time.

Aims and objectives

- To learn to draw o'clock on an analogue clock.

Resources

- Clock face
- Blank paper or invitation templates

Preparation

- Prepare the invitation templates if using.

What to do

- Explain to the children that they will be inviting one of their teddy bears to the picnic.
- Talk about the time the picnic will be held (two o'clock) and show the children two o'clock on the analogue clock.
- Encourage the children to create invitations (or complete the template) and include a diagram of the analogue clock on the invitation so their teddy knows what two o'clock looks like.

Tips

- **Vary the amount you have completed the template depending on the children's confidence or motivation in writing. Some children may prefer to draw a picture of their teddy.**
- **Some children will not have a teddy bear. Encourage the children to bring any toy of their choosing, explaining it does not have to be a teddy bear.**

Variations

- Use time-related invitations when the children are inviting people to come to talk to them, or when they are making notices about educational visits they are going on.
- Talk about the duration of the event to help the children to think also about the passing of time.

How is this maths?

Time can be seen in two different ways, passing the time and telling the time. Reading the time on an analogue clock is very complex and confusing. For example, an analogue clock reads ten minutes to twelve but when the minute hand is on the eight it is not eight minutes to the hour! Each hour is given by a number but the minutes are only shown by indentations. Fifteen minutes past can also be said as quarter past, but the hand points at three!

Preparing and making the picnic

The day is arriving! Let's get the picnic prepared.

Sandwich fillings

A data-collection task to ensure the children get their favourite sandwich at the picnic.

Aims and objectives

- To practise counting.
- To learn about data handling.

Resources

- Large pictures of the sandwich fillings on offer
- Sticky notes

Preparation

- Laminate the sandwich fillings pictures if you wish, to reuse when the sandwiches are being prepared.
- Write the children's names on the sticky notes, one per child

What to do

- Explain to the children that on the day of the picnic they will be making their sandwiches and so to ensure that everyone gets a sandwich they want to eat, we need to organise how many of each filling we need to buy.
- Show the children the filling options and display them clearly while they are being discussed. Ask the children to choose their favourite filling for their sandwich.
- Pass the children the sticky note with their name.

- Ask one child to identify their favourite filling. Give them the picture of that filling and ask them to stand in a designated area in the room. Repeat until all the pictures have been given out.
- Ask the remaining children to sit next to the person holding their favourite filling.
- The person holding the picture will take the sticky note from each child in turn and place it on the picture.
- Ask the groups to return one at a time and collate the information on a board. Talk about which is the *most popular* filling, which is the *least popular* and why that might be the case.
- Remind the children that they will be using the filling they have identified in their own sandwich.

Tip **Encourage the groups to check that the number of sticky notes they have corresponds to the number of children in their group.**

Variation

The children may write their own name on their sticky note. The activity could be undertaken in the same way as the data-handling activity in 'Travelling' (see pages 77–79), using a pictogram or block graph instead.

How is this maths?

The children are sorting the sandwich fillings and identifying how much of each filling is required. This is a type of data handling that helps them achieve a specific purpose and reduces waste.

Making the sandwiches

On the day of the picnic the children can make their own sandwiches.

Aims and objectives

- To follow instructions.
- To estimate quantity.

Resources

- Instructions on a recipe card (numbered, with illustrations)
- Bread
- Butter or spread
- Fillings
- Butter knives
- Cutting boards and plates
- Fillings cards with children's named sticky notes on them (from previous activity)

Preparation

- Set out the utensils, bread, butter and one filling and its instructions on each table.

What to do

- Demonstrate to the children how to make a sandwich by following the instructions on the recipe card:
  1. Lay the bread out.
  2. Butter the bread.
  3. Spread the jam (or whatever filling is on the table).
  4. Place the slices of bread together.
  5. Put the sandwich onto a plate.
- Remind the children that they are sharing the filling and butter with all the children at their table so they need to think carefully about how much they are taking.
- Identify which children will be working at which table.
- Send one group at a time to wash their hands.
- The children can then make their sandwich.
- Ask the children to place the sandwich on the plate with their named sticky note from the filling picture.

Tips

- **The more adults that are present the better support can be given to those children who may need a little extra help.**
- **As the children are following the numbered instructions encourage them to use *first*, *second*, and so on.**

Variations

- Make the toast with various spreads.
- Make porridge with various additions for a visit from Daddy Bear, Mummy Bear and Baby Bear.

How is this maths?

Following instructions such as those in a recipe helps children to think about *ordinal numbers* (first, second, third ...). The children are also *estimating* the quantities of butter and filling required to make their sandwich.

Shapely sandwiches

Children enjoy eating sandwiches that are made into novel shapes.

Aims and objectives

- To practise conserving area.
- To name different shapes.

Resources

- Sandwiches made in previous activity
- Selection of biscuit cutters

Preparation

- If not following this activity on from the previous one then make some sandwiches or toast some slices of bread for the children to cut.

What to do

- Discuss how children normally have their sandwiches cut. Draw examples on the board, or demonstrate with existing sandwiches. Talk about the shapes that are made (*right-angled triangles*, *squares*, *rectangles*).
- Explain that today the children are going to make different shapes using cutters.

- Show the children the selection of cutters that are available to them. Discuss the shapes they make.
- Demonstrate how to use a cutter safely (i.e. check the sharp side is on the bread and push down with a flat palm) and most effectively (i.e. ensure the position of the shape is carefully planned out to reduce waste and check that it has cut through completely before removing).
- Show one piece of bread cut with the cutter in the middle and show how few/no other shapes can now be made.

Do not discard some shapes because they are 'too hard' for the children. For example, the shape below is a *dodecagon* because it has 12 sides. The children will love learning the names of new shapes!

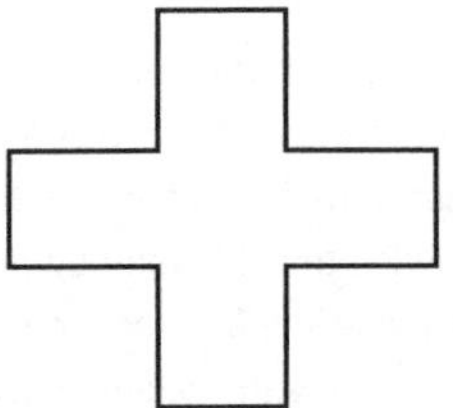

Variation

This activity can also work when the children are making biscuits. Roll out the biscuit dough and cut the shapes before baking.

How is this maths?

The children have to use their knowledge of *conservation of area* to choose the best place to use the cutters. By moving the cutters around until best use is made of the bread children will learn that what the cutter simply looks like can be deceptive in terms of how much space it uses!

It's a wrap!

Finally, the sandwiches need to be wrapped to take on the picnic.

Aims and objectives

- To estimate surface area.

Resources

- Sandwiches
- Greaseproof paper or similar for wrapping the sandwiches
- Small bags to place wrapped sandwiches in for carrying to the picnic

Preparation

- Cut the greaseproof paper into various sizes, some of which will not wrap a sandwich because they are too small and others that are too big and a waste of paper/wrapping.

What to do

- Place a selection of cut paper in the centre of each table.
- Encourage the children to take turns to look at the available paper and pick one piece to wrap their sandwich with.
- The other children can judge the child on how accurate their choice of paper was – was the paper too *big*, *too small*, or the *correct size*?
- Keep the named sticky notes with the sandwiches as they are placed in bags, one per child.

Tip **You may encourage the children to cut the paper themselves.**

Variation

Match different-sized wrapping paper to boxes, cups to bottles of water or icing to biscuits, and so on!

How is this maths?

Estimating the surface area of an object is tricky. This activity gives children practice at this using visual clues. The more they practise, the more accurate their estimates will become.

Chapter 9
Feet

Introduction

The activities in this chapter could be planned and organised as a component of the 'All about me' activities in Chapter 6, or run alone. In addition to thinking about their own feet, the children could also explore the feet of other animals and think about why those feet are adapted to include certain features. In some cultures exposing feet to others can be insulting so be careful to know the children in your class before carrying out these activities.

My feet

Children love to compare their feet with other children's feet.

Aims and objectives

- To compare length.
- To understand ordering.

Resources

- Blank sheets of paper (or 2cm-squared paper – optional)
- Crayon or felt tips
- Scissors

Preparation

- Ask the children to remove their footwear if appropriate, or they can keep their shoes on if they wish.

What to do

- Ask each child to stand still on the paper while you (or their friend) draw around their foot.
- The children can cut out their foot or leave it on the sheet.
- Encourage the children to order the feet in some way, for example from *longest* to *shortest*.

Children are likely to find they are ticklish when their feet are drawn around, so be sympathetic to this. If you use 2cm-squared paper the children can compare the area of their feet by counting the squares. Smaller squares are more difficult to keep an accurate count of.

Variation

Draw around hands or whole bodies.

How is this maths?

Children are able to *compare* their foot with other feet. *Indirect comparison* occurs when children know that if child A's foot is shorter than child B's, and child B's foot is shorter than child C's, then child A's foot must be shorter than child C's. The term for this was coined by Piaget: *transitivity*. It underpins a lot of logical reasoning in mathematics.

Shoe sizes

Let's take a look at our shoe sizes.

Aims and objectives

- To use numbers in measurement contexts.

Resources

- A shoe sizer known as a Brannock Device®, from a shoe shop (optional)

Preparation

- None required.

What to do

- Ask the children to take off their shoes and identify their shoe size by reading it on the shoe.
- Order the shoes according to size. Ask, 'Who has the biggest shoe? Who has the middle-sized shoe? How would we work that out?'. (Encourage counting from the outsides to find the middle shoe or shoes if there is an even number of shoes.)
- Talk about what size is – does it mean longest or widest or both?
- Ask, 'What is shoe size?'

Tip The discussion may move into width if, for example, the shoe size is 5F as the alphanumeric system includes a width indicator.

Variation

You might talk about how shoe sizes revert to size 1 after size 13!

How is this maths?

Talking about shoe size gives children an opportunity to talk about numbers in another context. While it is still *standardised*, shoe size is a measurement that the children will use less regularly.

Types of shoes

Sort the shoes for the role-play shoe shop.

Aims and objectives

- To sort and classify.

Resources

- Shoe shop role-play area
- Selection of shoes
- Shoe boxes
- Shelving in the role-play area for shoe display and storage

Preparation

- No preparation required if the role-play area has been set up previously.

What to do

- Explain to the children that the shop has had another delivery of shoes but they have been mixed up.
- Can the children sort them and make labels on the shelves for the different types of shoes?
- During and after the sorting, talk to the children about the decisions they made. Ask questions such as 'What groups have you arranged the shoes into? Are there any shoes that do not fit those groups? What are you going to do with them? How are you planning to arrange the groups in the storage area? What labels are you making?'
- Encourage some customers to come into the shop to comment on the arrangement of the shoes in the shop. Ask, 'What do you like about the categories the shoe salespeople have arranged the shoes into? Would you have done it any differently? Why?'

Allow the children to come up with their own methods of sorting the shoes. Categories might include colour, practical use, season, materials made from, like/dislike and size.

Variation

Any objects can be sorted, depending on the topic/theme being followed. For example, when looking at 'Jack and the Beanstalk' the children might sort a number of seeds, or when learning about food the children might sort according to types of food.

How is this maths?

Being able to categorise items into manageable groups is an important aspect of handling data. Being able to group numbers later on helps to solve more difficult calculation problems.

Trying shoes on

Select your shoes from the role-play shop and buy them today!

Aims and objectives

- To use language related to size.
- To recognise amounts written down.
- To recognise coins and notes.

Resources

- Selection of children's shoes (ask all the children to bring in a named pair of their own)
- Shoe measurer (Brannock Device®) from a shoe shop (optional)
- Price labels for shoes
- Bags to put the new purchases in
- Play money
- Till

Preparation

- The role-play area will have been set up prior to this activity. Make price labels with the children displaying the price they think the shoes should be charged at.

What to do

- Encourage children to enter the role-play area. Some will be the shop assistants and others will be customers.
- Once in role the children will serve or be served in the shop by trying on a number of shoes, listening to recommendations and feedback about size.
- Once an appropriate shoe has been identified, the children can purchase that pair.

Tip Encourage the children to use vocabulary such as *size*, *big*, *tight*, *small*, *width*.

Variation

This type of activity can happen in other shop role-play areas, such as trying on clothes, hats or gloves.

How is this maths?

The children are using mathematical language to explain the shape and size of shoes, comparing them to their feet. Although the amounts of money exchanged are unlikely to be realistic at this stage, they are using number in a context that is meaningful to them.

Boxes

Putting shoes in boxes that match the size and colour labels.

Aims and objectives

- To learn about sorting.
- To practise logical thinking.

Resources

- A selection of laminated pictures of shoes that are in a range of colours and styles (suggested criteria below):

	Pair A	Pair B	Pair C	Pair D	Pair E	Pair F	Pair G	Pair H
Size	Adult	Adult	Adult	Adult	Child	Child	Child	Child
Colour	Blue	Red	Green	Yellow	Blue	Red	Green	Yellow
Fastening	Velcro	Velcro	Laces	Laces	Velcro	Velcro	Laces	Laces
Season	Summer	Winter	Summer	Winter	Summer	Winter	Summer	Winter

- Shoe boxes that are labelled according to the shoes (these 'boxes' may be labelled envelopes or similar)

Sample labels:

ADULT

Adult/Child: ADULT

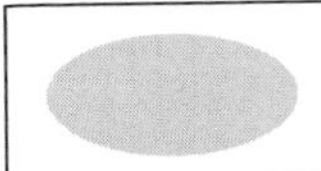

Colour: BLUE

Fastening: LACES

Season: WINTER

Preparation

- Make up the shoe cards (see suggested table in 'Resources' section above).

What to do

- Display the boxes with their labels.
- Encourage the children either to a) choose one box and find the shoes that meet the criteria on the box labels, or b) choose any pair of shoes and then identify the box that they belong to.

Tips

- **You do not have to label the boxes with all of the criteria you have designed.**
- **If you are designing your own criteria, plan the shoes logically if you want to use the same cards again to play the game in the next section (see 'Guess who?' below).**

Variations

- The children may want to design their own shoes that meet the criteria on the box. If these are laminated they can be used as part of the game by other children.
- Any context can be used. For example, (fictitious) insects can be made according to size, patternation on back, number of eyes, length of legs and so on. Trees can be created according to height, colour, leaf shape and so on. Dinosaurs can be created according to length, height and weight, dietary requirements and so on. The important thing to remember is that there is an identifiable logic to the design.

How is this maths?

The children are applying *logical reasoning* to solve the problem. They are identifying whether the shoe meets or does not meet the criteria.

Guess who?

Identify which shoe is missing from the set.

Aims and objectives

- To practise logical thinking.

Resources

- The shoe cards from the 'Boxes' activity above
- Labels from the boxes (optional)

Preparation

- If the cards have already been made there is no further preparation required.

What to do

- Place all the shoe cards face up on the table. Ensure the attributes of the shoes are known to the group.
- Two children leave the group while the remainder of the children remove one of the cards. Shuffle them around so that it is not immediately obvious where the card has been taken from.
- When the children return, they need to identify the attributes of the missing shoes. (This is where the labels from the boxes may be useful as an *aide-mémoire* for the pair.)
- Once the shoes have been identified, the game starts over with a new pair of children.

Tips

- **Play this game only when the children have played 'Boxes' for some time. They need to be familiar with the shoes and their attributes for the game to be successful.**
- **You may begin by playing with a smaller number of shoes (i.e. using only children's shoes will halve the number of shoes in the set and make it easier).**

Variation

See Variations in 'Boxes'.

How is this maths?

In order to solve the puzzle the children must apply *logical thinking* in order to identify which *attribute* is missing. Logical thinking is a prerequisite for problem solving and mathematical investigations later on.

Pairs

Aims and objectives

- To practise counting in twos.
- To use 'pair' to indicate two.

Resources

- Cards with the numbers 1, 3, 5, 7, 9, 11, 13, 15, 17 and 19 on them in one colour, e.g. black
- Cards with the numbers 2, 4, 6, 8, 10, 12, 14, 16, 18 and 20 on them in a second colour, e.g. red
- Ten pairs of shoes

Preparation

- Line up the shoes in pairs.

What to do

- Ask the children what they notice about the shoes (elicit responses such as 'they are in twos').
- Ask the children to count the shoes (1, 2, 3, 4 and so on).
- Place a number card above each shoe as it is counted.
- Encourage the children to think about another way to count the shoes (i.e. in twos).
- Count in twos, pointing to the even number cards. Ask the children, 'What do you notice?'
- Repeat counting in twos. As the children see the connection with the second shoe of each pair and the even numbers, begin to remove the odd number cards.
- If appropriate after a while remove some of the even-number cards when counting, to encourage the children to think about the number pattern and help them begin to memorise it.

Tips

- Encourage the children to use the term *pair* when talking about two shoes.
- The children will be making the link between the *enactive* (physical) and the *symbolic* (numerals) because you are bringing together the shoes and the number cards.
- What patterns can the children see?

Variations

- To extend this ask, 'I have three pairs of shoes, so how many shoes do I have altogether?'
- You can practise counting in fives by using children holding up their hands, or pictures of hands, showing five fingers. Counting in tens can be achieved by using two hands. Counting in threes can be done using tricycle pictures (counting the wheels) and counting in fours using animals (counting four legs).

How is this maths?

Counting in twos is a prerequisite to learning the two-times table with understanding.

Have you got sole?

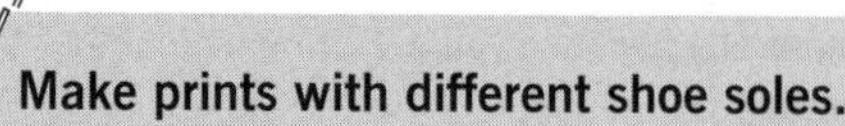

Make prints with different shoe soles.

Aims and objectives

- To recognise and discuss symmetry and pattern.

Resources

- Variety of old boots and shoes that have interesting and varied soles
- A variety of paints and large shallow trays to pour them into
- Large sheets of paper or cardboard for printing on
- Art aprons
- Old newspaper
- Washing bowls for dipping shoe soles in when changing colour
- Old towels for drying off washed soles

Preparation

- Ensure the floor is covered with newspaper or plastic that can be cleaned.
- Secure large sheets of paper onto the floor.
- Set out the paints into large shallow trays (large enough for the boot soles to be placed in and covered with paint).

What to do

- Talk to the children about the patterns they can see and feel on the soles of the shoes. Do they see a difference in the types of soles depending on the type of shoe? (For example a boot may have a thicker sole and deeper grooves compared to a slipper, which may be a lot thinner and smoother.)
- Explain that they are going to use a range of colours and shoes to make a printed picture. Talk about how the different soles will create different textures and how the children can use different soles and colours for different elements of their prints.

- Demonstrate how the children can print using the soles. Identify where soles with the same colour paint on them can go, and show them how to clean a sole of its paint if they want to change the colour.
- The children may design their print first, or they may create it as they go!

Tips

- **This activity is best undertaken in pairs or small groups of children around a large sheet of paper.**
- **Encourage the children to talk about the pattern and the texture of each sole as they work to design and print their art.**
- **Encourage the children to identify *parallel lines*, *zigzags*, *circles*, *waves* and other geometrical shapes, as well as *thin*, *thick*, *long*, *short* and so on.**

Variation

Use other items to provide different textures, depending on any theme or topic.

How is this maths?

The children are using geometrical language to describe the patterns they observe on the soles.

Chapter 10
Songs and chants

Introduction

Children love to sing and chant. The songs in this chapter are all related to mathematical concepts, such as counting forwards and backwards, counting in twos, exploring shape and positional language. It is also possible to explore these ideas through story and rhyme and often you will find story books that retell the songs. Leaving out a CD player with a microphone and/or headsets will encourage children to sing along during continual provision and to perform to others.

1, 2, 3, 4, 5

Use fish for counting and learning left and right.

Aims and objectives

- To practise counting to ten.
- To identify left and right.

Resources

- Backing music (optional)

Preparation

- If you are not sure of the tune, find the song using an internet search of the first line of the lyrics.

What to do

- Sing the song through together, showing the ten fingers as the numbers are counted.
- Show the little finger on the right hand when singing the last line.

Lyrics

One, two, three, four, five,
Once I caught a fish alive.
Six, seven, eight, nine, ten,
Then I put it back again.
'Why did you let it go?'
Because it bit my finger so
'Which finger did it bite?'
This little finger on the right.

Ensure that the children are holding up their right hand to show their 'little finger on the right'.

Variation

Other counting songs include 'This old man' ('he played one, he played knick knack on my drum') and 'The pirate song' ('When I was one I'd just begun the day I went to sea').

How is this maths?

The children are practising counting and identifying their right little finger. Counting develops into *addition*, and knowing right from left is important when giving and following directions later on.

One elephant came out to play

Elephants can help us to remember how to count!

Aims and objectives

- To practise counting.
- To learn how to use 'one more'.

Resources

- Backing music (optional)

Preparation

- If you are not sure of the tune, find the song using an internet search of the first line of the lyrics.

What to do

- Ask the children to sit in a circle.
- Identify one child to be the elephant. That child plays and dances, as if they are on a spider's web, in the space in the middle of the circle.
- Sing the song (see words below).

Lyrics

One elephant went out to play upon a spider's web one day.
S/he thought it such tremendous fun that s/he called for another elephant to come.

- When the song says that the elephant *called for another elephant to come*, the first child chooses another child to come into the middle.
- Continue as long as space allows.

Pause the singing as each elephant joins, and count how many elephants there are now.

Variations

- Use pictures of elephants that children place on a spider's web made of string as the song progresses. You may also write or show the numerals representing the number of elephants on the spider's web.
- Draw a card out of a pile to show how many more elephants have been invited! The lyrics would be, for example:
  Six elephants went out to play upon a spider's web one day.
  They thought it such tremendous fun that they called for another three elephants to come.
- Work out how many elephants are on the web altogether.

How is this maths?

Inviting one more elephant to play models *adding one more*. Knowing the number that is *one more* helps children understand the *counting numbers* and the concept of *counting on*. This is early addition.

Ten green bottles

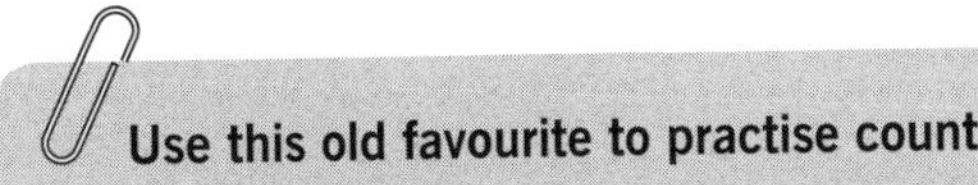

Use this old favourite to practise counting backwards.

Aims and objectives

- To practise counting backwards.
- To understand taking away one at a time.

Resources

- Ten green bottles (or pictures of them) numbered 1–10
- Backing music (optional)

Preparation

- If you are not sure of the tune, find the song using an internet search of the first line of the lyrics.
- Set up the bottles in a row.

What to do

- Start singing the song (see lyrics below). When the song reaches one bottle accidentally falling, remove one bottle or picture.
- Keep singing until all the bottles are gone.

Lyrics

Ten green bottles hanging on the wall,
Ten green bottles hanging on the wall,
And if one green bottle should accidentally fall,
There'll be nine green bottles hanging on the wall.

Nine green bottles hanging on the wall,
Nine green bottles hanging on the wall
And if one green bottle should accidentally fall,
There'll be eight green bottles hanging on the wall.

Eight green bottles hanging on the wall.
Eight green bottles hanging on the wall.

And if one ...

... There'll be one green bottle hanging on the wall.

One green bottle hanging on the wall,
One green bottle hanging on the wall.

And if that green bottle should accidentally fall,
There'll be no green bottles hanging on the wall.

Tip **Remove the bottle with the highest number on it each time. This will show the correct number of remaining bottles. Count them to check.**

Variations

- Other items related to the theme or topic being studied can be substituted for the green bottles.
- Other songs that encourage *counting backwards* in ones include, 'Five currant buns' ('in a baker's shop'), 'Five little speckled frogs' ('sat on a speckled log'), 'Five little ducks' ('went swimming one day'), 'Ten in the bed' ('and the little one said "roll over, roll over"') and 'Five little men in a flying saucer' ('flew round the Earth one day').

How is this maths?

Counting backwards is an early entry into *subtraction* and *taking away* one. Knowing that no green bottles exist helps children understand that it is possible to count backwards to zero, but that we begin at one when we start counting.

Ten fat sausages

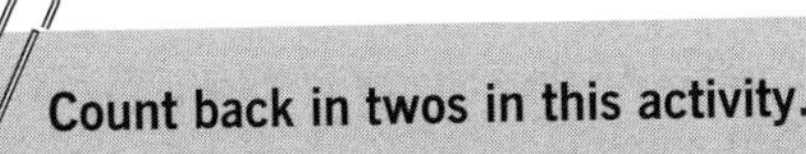

Aims and objectives

- To take away two.

Resources

- Backing music (optional)

Preparation

- If you are not sure of the tune, find the song using an internet search of the first line of the lyrics.

What to do

- Identify ten children to volunteer to be the sausages sizzling in the pan. Ask them to stand at the front.
- Start singing the song (see lyrics below). When the song reaches the point that one sausage goes 'pop' the first child sits down where they are and as another sausage goes 'bang' the second child also sits down.

Lyrics

Ten fat sausages sizzling in the pan,
Ten fat sausages sizzling in the pan.
If one went pop and the other went bang,
There'd be eight fat sausages sizzling in the pan,
Eight fat sausages, sizzling in the pan ...

- Sing until all the sausages (children) are sitting down.

Tips

- **Identify the order in which the sausages (children) will go 'pop' and 'bang' (i.e. sit down) before you start, to help maintain the momentum once the song has begun.**
- **Give some time between verses for the children to work out how many sausages are left in the pan.**
- **Practise counting in twos.**

Variation

The sausages sizzling in the pan can be changed to a current topic. For example, 'ten balloons floating in the sky'.

How is this maths?

Counting backwards is an early entry into *subtraction* and this song encourages *taking away* two. Knowing that no sausages exist helps children understand that it is possible to count backwards to zero, but that we begin at one when we start counting.

I'm a circle

Sing these lyrics to the well-known tune of 'Frère Jacques'.

Aims and objectives

- To explore some properties of circles.

Resources

- Circular or spherical objects to roll (optional)

Preparation

- If you are not sure of the tune, find it using an internet search of the lyrics 'Are you sleeping, are you sleeping, Brother John?'

What to do

- Sing the song together (see lyrics below).
- The children can use their 'magic fingers' to draw circles in the air or roll circular objects to each other around or across the room.

Lyrics

I'm a circle, I'm a circle,
Big and round, big and round.
I can roll to you and I can roll to you,
Along the ground, along the ground.

If using circular objects, select as varied a range of objects as possible.

Variation

In later verses substitute 'circle' with the name of an object such as 'round wheel' or 'sphere' (for a ball).

How is this maths?

Children need to learn that shapes have a number of properties. By singing that a circle is round, they are learning about its *curved side*. By singing that the *sphere* is round, they are learning about its *curved face*. Providing the children with a range of objects helps to extend their understanding of the properties of shapes and ensures that their view of them does not become limited to one or two instantiations (examples).

The farm is shaping up

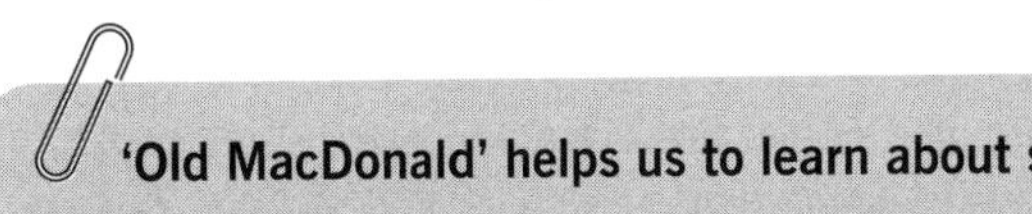

'Old MacDonald' helps us to learn about shape.

Aims and objectives

- To use properties to identify two-dimensional shapes.

Resources

- A deck of cards with a shape drawn on one side
- A feely bag large enough to hold the cards

Preparation

- Shuffle the cards and place them into the feely bag.
- If you are not sure of the tune, find the song 'Old MacDonald Had a Farm' using an internet search of the song title.

What to do

- Select one child to draw one card out of the bag and say the spoken line in the song when appropriate (see lyrics below).
- Sing the song together.

Lyrics

In this bag I have a shape, I wonder what it is?

Will you help me to find out just what shape it is?

(Spoken) It has ___ corners and ____ sides

(Sung) So, do you know what shape this is? Tell me if you do!

- The child who gives the spoken clues responds to the children's guesses of what shape it is with 'yes' or 'no'.

Tips

- **Draw the shapes on the cards in different orientations and colours to challenge children's notion that shapes can only be a particular prototypical shape (e.g. a *triangle* can only be a triangle when it is *equilateral* and has a *horizontal baseline*).**
- **Write the name of the shape on the card as well as drawing the figure.**

Variation

Use photos or pictures of three-dimensional solids for the children to describe, or place a solid in the feely bag for the child to feel and give the properties (number of *corners* or *vertices* and *faces*).

How is this maths?

Children need to learn that shapes have a number of properties. In this singing game children will use two-dimensional geometric vocabulary such as *corners* and *sides*. If playing a three-dimensional version they will use *vertex*, *vertices* and *faces*.

Positional language

Lots of songs help us to use positional language.

Aims and objectives

- To use accurate positional language.

Resources

- Backing music (optional)

Preparation

- If you are not sure of the tunes, find the songs using an internet search of the lyrics.

What to do

- Sing a range of songs that use positional language. These include:

The grand old Duke of York,
He had ten thousand men.
He marched them *up* to the *top* of the hill
And he marched them *down* again.
And when they were *up* they were *up*,
And when they were *down* they were *down*,
And when they were only *halfway up*
They were neither *up* nor *down*.

Humpty Dumpty sat *on* a wall.
Humpty Dumpty had a great fall.
All the king's horses and all the king's men
Couldn't put Humpty together again.

Jack and Jill went *up* the hill
to fetch a pail of water.
Jack fell *down* and broke his crown
and Jill came tumbling after.

Up Jack got and home did trot
as fast as he could caper.
He went to bed and bound his head
with vinegar and brown paper.

Ring, a ring o' roses,
A pocket full of posies;
Atishoo, atishoo,
We all fall *down*.

- Where appropriate the children can act out the positional language.

Tip **Keep the positional language (italicised in the lyrics above) in your mind so you are accenting these words when you sing them with the children.**

Variation

Watch videos of these traditional nursery rhymes or ask the children to use puppets to act out the rhymes.

How is this maths?

Using positional language helps children to make sense of shape and space and supports their geometrical thinking.

Chapter 11
Mathematical walks

Introduction

We learn mathematics to help us to make sense of the world, and so exploring further afield while we think about mathematics is a fun activity to undertake with children. The walks that have been suggested in this chapter are offered as a starting point. As you walk about in your area you may well find other mathematical ideas you can explore with the children. It is also possible to stay inside to carry out several of these activities if you prefer.

As small as small can be

How small can your collection be?

Aims and objectives

- To use language related to size.

Resources

- Very small containers, enough for one per child or pair of children

Preparation

- Go on the designated walk yourself to check that it is safe for the children and that there are enough items that can be collected on the way.

What to do

- Give the children the containers. Ask them, 'What things can you think of that are small enough to go into your box?'. Share ideas.
- On the walk challenge the children to find five things to put into the box.
- On your return compare the contents by asking about who has the same things and which things are different.

Tip

Ensure you have discussed health and safety matters with the children as well as the need for respect for neighbours and living things.

Variation

Use one box per adult-led group to potentially generate more discussion during the walk.

How is this maths?

The children are visualising items that might be smaller than the box. The children are using trial and error as they try objects in the box. The children are finding similarities and differences in the objects found. They are using language such as *too big* and *that fits* as they explore their surroundings.

A head for heights

This walk encourages children to think about objects that are taller or shorter than they are.

Aims and objectives

- To estimate height.
- To compare using non-standard units.

Resources

- Digital camera

Preparation

- Go on the designated walk yourself to check that it is safe for the children and that there are enough items that can be photographed on the way.

What to do

- Explain to the children that you are going on a walk together to find objects that are *taller* and *shorter* than the children.
- Think about some of the objects that you might see on the way. List those on the board or a sheet of paper.
- Undertake the walk, photographing objects that are seen on the way with a child next to each to show if the object is *taller* or *shorter* than the child.
- On your return show the digital photos on the interactive whiteboard and discuss which objects are taller and which are shorter than the children.

Ensure you have discussed health and safety matters with the children as well as respect for neighbours and living things.

Variation

Print out some of the photos from the walk. In another session encourage the children to group the objects into taller and shorter. Encourage them to discuss if the object will remain the same height or change, and why.

How is this maths?

The children are using their *estimation* skills and then *direct comparison* by placing themselves next to an object and photographing it.

Shape hunt

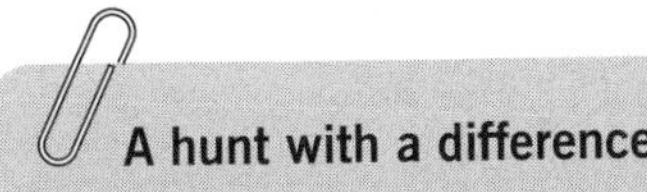

A hunt with a difference.

Aims and objectives

- To observe different shapes within the environment.

Resources

- A set of cards in a small pouch the children can each carry around their neck, or in an envelope they can carry – one set each or per pair

Preparation

- Go on the designated walk yourself to check that it is safe for the children and that there are enough items on the way that will meet the criteria.

What to do

- Before setting off, talk to the children about the shapes in their pack. Ensure the children can say the names (e.g. *sphere*, *rectangular prism*, *cylinder*).
- Photograph the objects that the children see.
- On the group's return view the photos on the interactive whiteboard to discuss.

Ensure you have discussed health and safety matters with the children, as well as having respect for neighbours and living things.

Variations

- Print off the photos and display them on the wall. Include on the display the mathematical terms alongside the names of the everyday objects.

- The packs may also include drawings of two-dimensional shapes, such as *triangle*, *circle*, *rectangle* but if this is the case ensure that it is the *face* of the object that is being photographed and discussed so that the brick that is a rectangular prism doesn't become known as a rectangle.

How is this maths?

The children are using their visualisation skills to imagine and observe three-dimensional shapes in their environment. They discuss their findings with their friends using accurate terminology in order to develop their mathematical communication skills.

A focus on one shape

Explore a shape of the day.

Aims and objectives

- To observe shape being used in the environment.

Resources

- None required

Preparation

- Go on the designated walk yourself to check that it is safe for the children and that there are enough items on the way that will meet the criteria.

What to do

- Before setting off talk to the children about the 'shape of the day', e.g. circle.
- During the walk ask, 'What circles can you see?'
- Identify whether the circles are the face of another shape (a wheel, a kind of circular prism) or a sphere (a ball).
- The children could draw what they have seen on their return, to create a display about their 'shape of the day'.

Tips

- Ensure you have discussed health and safety matters with the children, as well as respect for neighbours and living things.
- The shape could be the 'shape of the week' or even the 'shape of the month'!
- Ensure you show the children a number of different ways the shape can be used, to broaden their understanding of what the shape looks like and how it can be used in the environment.

Variation

Encourage the children to bring into nursery/school examples of objects or toys that have the 'shape of the day' in them.

How is this maths?

The children are using their *visualisation* skills to imagine and observe three-dimensional shapes in their environment. They discuss their findings with their friends using accurate vocabulary in order to develop their mathematical *communication* skills.

Colour

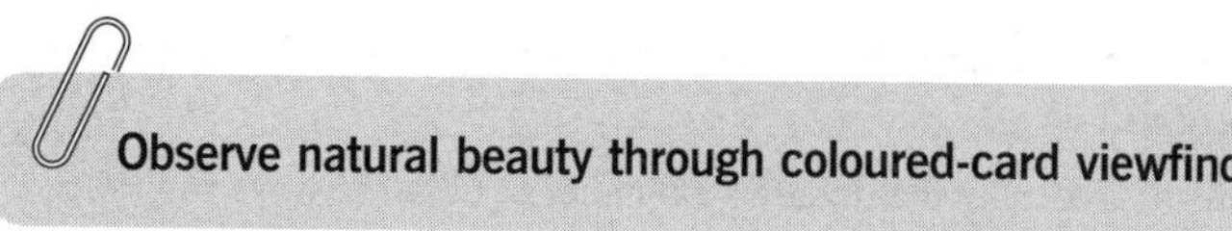

Observe natural beauty through coloured-card viewfinders.

Aims and objectives

- To identify colours.
- To categorise colours.

Resources

- Coloured cards with a circular hole cut out of the centre, enough for three per child

Preparation

- Laminate the coloured cards after the hole has been made in the card to make the cards sturdy and reuseable.
- Go on the designated walk yourself to check that it is safe for the children and that there are enough items on the way that will meet the criteria.

What to do

- Ask the children to find items on the walk that are the same colour as the cards they have.
- Discuss the colour and photograph the object.

Tips

- **Looking through the hole will help identify the object's colour.**
- **Ensure you have discussed health and safety matters with the children, as well as respect for neighbours and living things.**

Variation

If items are photographed they can be printed out and displayed on the wall; perhaps make a rainbow, or group the objects according to their colour.

How is this maths?

Although colour might be thought of as art or design more than mathematics, mathematics (ratio) is used to mix colours. Assigning an object a certain colour categorises that object. Colour is used in science (horticulture) to order some flowers. There is also a science and mathematics link to draw when looking at how prisms refract (bend) light at different angles causing different colours.

Texture

Go on a walk that provides the opportunity to touch and feel various objects.

Aims and objectives

- To sort objects according to texture.

Resources

- Texture cards or a list of textures (optional)

Preparation

- Go on the designated walk yourself to check that it is safe for the children and that there are enough items on the way that will meet the criteria.

What to do

- Find items that are smooth, rough, cold, soft, spongy, dry and so on.
- Collect or photograph them.
- On return to the nursery/classroom, sort the objects into texture groups.
- Display.

Tip Ensure you have discussed health and safety matters with the children, as well as respect for neighbours and living things.

Variation

Ask the children to bring in objects that have the particular textures you are looking for.

How is this maths?

The children *classify* and *group* the objects according to their properties (texture).

Chapter 12
Pirates

Introduction

'Pirates' is always a favourite topic with young children. The activities in this chapter help you to think about how to exploit the mathematical ideas within the types of activities you might normally carry out when undertaking this theme. Activities such as map making and map reading can be undertaken indoors or out, on a smaller scale or larger, depending on the space you have available to you. You could turn the whole classroom into a treasure island, or use the role-play area, or create a temporary island on a carpet area.

A living treasure island

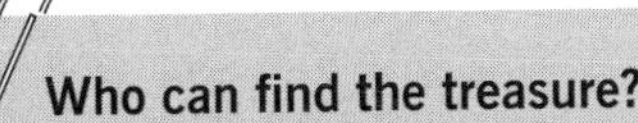

Who can find the treasure?

Aims and objectives

- To give and follow directions.

Resources

- Items to transform an area into a treasure island (e.g. hoops, coloured paper, 'treasure')
- Labels for north, south, east and west

Preparation

- Develop the treasure island with the children.

What to do

- The children are sitting around or on the treasure island.
- One child is selected to leave the area.
- The remainder of children hide treasure (such as gold coins) under objects on the island.
- The child returns to be given directions about where to find the buried treasure.

Use however many paces north, south, east or west to provide directions.

Variation

Instead of using *compass directions*, use paces towards particular items on the treasure island.

How is this maths?

This type of activity encourages children to make sense of the space around them. Later on they begin to use *coordinates*.

Treasure maps

X marks the spot!

Aims and objectives

- To give directions.

Resources

- Blank map template (optional)
- Paper
- Pencils and colours

Preparation

- The previous activity, 'A living treasure island', is a good preparatory task for this activity.
- Look at a range of treasure maps from pirate books such as *The Night Pirates* by Peter Harris and Deborah Allwright or *Stories of Pirates* by Russell Punter and Christyan Fox.

What to do

- Encourage the children to draw their own treasure maps, either of an island they are familiar with or their own imaginary island.
- X marks the spot – where is the treasure?
- Ask, 'What else is on the map?' and 'How can you get from the cove to the treasure?'
- Encourage the children to talk about their maps and put a key on them to explain the symbols used.

Tip You could make the maps look old by dipping them into cold tea and screwing them up!

Variation

Other themes or topics also lend themselves to making maps. For example, the children may want to draw maps showing their journey from home to nursery/school, the park, a relative's house or the local shop.

How is this maths?

The children are beginning to translate the three-dimensional world into a two-dimensional representation using symbols and a key to explain them. Later they will learn other symbols to develop the concept of maps further. The children are also able to explain and follow directions to and from particular points on the map. This demonstrates clear logical thinking.

Message in a bottle

Send the treasure map away.

Aims and objectives

- To practise estimation.
- To check results.

Resources

- A number of dry plastic bottles of all different shapes and sizes, more than one per child

Preparation

- Ensure that there are enough bottles for each child.

What to do

- Discuss how treasure maps were traditionally placed in bottles for safe keeping from water and the sea.
- Ask the children how they think the maps were put into the bottles (i.e. rolled up).

- Allow the children, in small groups at a time, to select a bottle they think their map will fit into.
- Check by rolling and inserting the map.
- Allow the children to change the bottle if necessary.

Tip **Before they have checked the bottle's suitability talk to the children about why they have selected that particular bottle.**

Variation

Encourage the children to work in pairs so they are able to talk about their estimations more effectively.

How is this maths?

The children are visualising their map in the bottle. They are required to *visualise* it rolled up and to take into consideration the *length* of the bottle and map, as well as how tightly the map can be rolled in relation to the size of the bottle's neck. This involves a lot of *conservation of surface area*.

Treasure chest

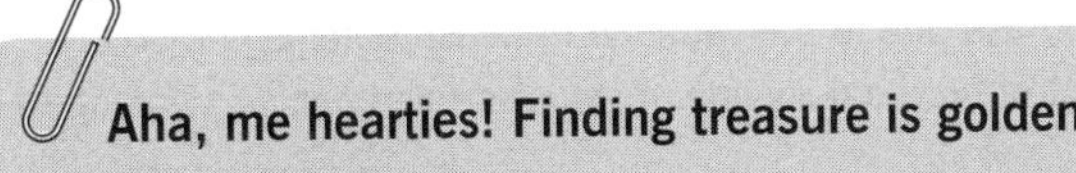

Aims and objectives

- To learn about problem solving.
- To learn about sharing.

Resources

- A treasure chest (can be a box covered in gold-coloured paper with a lid)
- Treasure (chocolate gold coins or costume jewellery)
- Balance scales (for helping the children to share out using weight)

Preparation

- Ensure that the treasure in the box can be shared evenly between the number of children in the group.

What to do

- Explore what is in the box.
- Ask, 'How much treasure is there?'.
- Ask, 'How can we *share* the treasure *equally* between us? Is there another way? And another way?' Discuss ways to share until there is general agreement between the 'pirates'.
- Talk to the children about how they know they are sharing equally as they carry out the sharing process.

The children might count or weigh some items of treasure (e.g. the chocolate coins). They may need to exchange some of their items (e.g. one necklace is worth two bracelets).

Variation

Use other objects related to a current theme or topic.

How is this maths?

The children are developing their understanding of *division as equal sharing*. This may be a difficult task due to the variation in treasure items and so the children will have a lot of *problem solving*, *negotiation* and *logical thinking* to undertake.

A pirate investigation

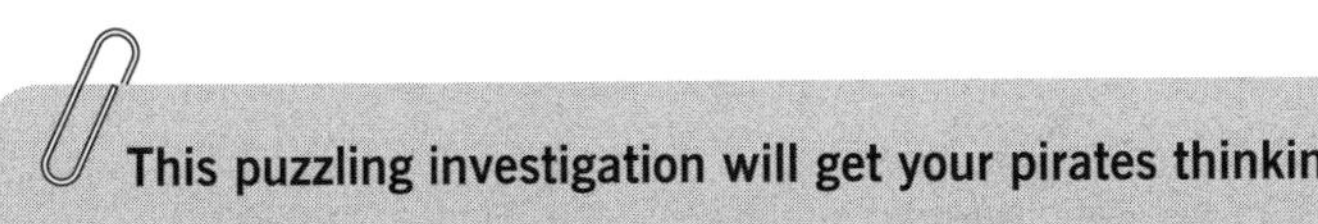

This puzzling investigation will get your pirates thinking!

Aims and objectives

- To practise logical thinking and reasoning.
- To learn about communication.
- To practise problem solving and investigating.

Resources

- Three sets of: pirate hat, eye patch, cutlass (each set is a different colour from the other two).
- Crayons, coloured pencils or felt tips the same colours as the three sets
- Recording sheet (optional, see Preparation below)

Preparation

- If encouraging the children to use the recording sheet, photocopy sets of hat, eye patch and cutlass so that there are eight sets on one side of A4 paper.

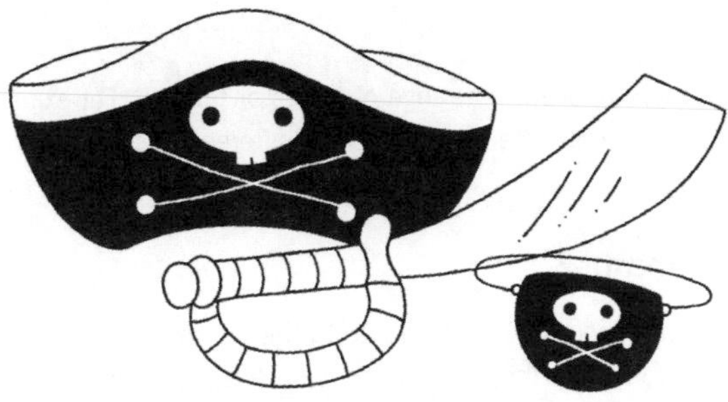

What to do

- Ask for one volunteer who is going to be a confused pirate.
- Show the pirate the box and ask them to pick out one hat, one eye patch and one cutlass and put them on.

- Reveal what else is in the box and ask them to change one, two or three of the items they are wearing. Repeat as many times as you think is necessary for the children to understand that there are many options for the confused pirate.
- Ask the children, 'How many different outfits can the confused pirate wear?'
- Working in pairs the children can investigate this question.
- Using the recording sheet (by colouring in the items using the three colours) helps the children to keep track of what they are discussing.
- Discuss conclusions at the end, asking the confused pirate to dress up again if necessary.

Tips

- **Once the children think they have identified all the possibilities, encourage them to check in a logical (*systematic*) way. One possible way to do that is to start with all the same-colour items, then change only one object at a time, then two and finally three.**
- **With younger children you may want to start with just two sets (colours).**

Variation

This activity can be applied to a range of topics or themes. For example, in a topic about winter the children can use three different sets comprising a hat, scarf and gloves.

How is this maths?

This investigation encourages the children to think through a problem in a *systematic* way to ensure they have all *possibilities* covered. This skill is an essential investigative approach to foster in children.

Ahoy there!

Build your own pirate ship.

Aims and objectives

- To understand estimation.
- To check estimations with direct comparison.

Resources

- Role play area or construction area
- Resources for making a pirate ship
- Pictures of and books with pirate ships

Preparation

- If necessary, prepare the areas where the children will be building their pirate ship(s).

What to do

- If appropriate, give the children the option of building a pirate ship together in the role play area or independently/in pairs in the construction area.
- Discuss what a pirate ship needs (e.g. flagpole, plank, bird's nest) by gaining inspiration from books and pictures.
- During the construction phase, ask questions such as 'How many planks (strips of paper to attach to the wall) do we need?' and 'What shape are you using there?'

Tip

Provide a variety of pictures of pirate ships so the children can identify common features to include in their ship design without being (too) stereotypical of pirates.

Variation

The role-play and construction areas can be used to build any construction related to the current topic or theme.

How is this maths?

The children will be selecting materials to use, *estimating* how much of the material to use, using it and checking the reasonableness of their estimation. If necessary they will use another piece. This *trial-and-error* approach to problem solving is used throughout mathematics.

The Jolly Roger

Create and then fly the pirate flag.

Aims and objectives

- To recognise reflective symmetry.

Resources

- A4 paper – black and white
- White-coloured pencils
- Scissors
- Glue

Preparation

- Produce a template of half a Jolly Roger, if required

What to do

- Hand out the black paper to the children and ask them to fold it in half.
- Encourage the children to draw half a Jolly Roger with a white-coloured pencil, using the template if required.
- Cut out the skull and crossbones, keeping the eyes and nose as they fall out.
- Open out the black paper.
- Stick the black paper onto the white paper.
- Fly the flags on the pirate ships or display them in the room.

Tips

- **Discuss why the two sides of the flag look the same and how that relates to folding the paper in half.**
- **This is a difficult task for children so ensure that there are lots of adults about to lend a hand.**

Variation

Different themes encourage different types of symmetrical patterns to be cut out and glued onto a contrasting background. One popular task is the snowflake, where blue paper can be cut and glued onto white, or vice versa.

How is this maths?

It is important for children to learn about symmetry because this will help them later to define shapes.

A pirate's life for me

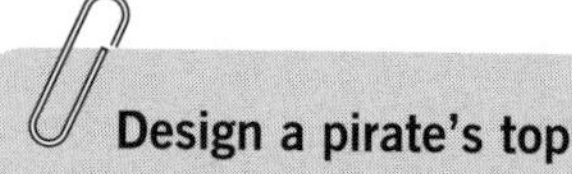

Design a pirate's top.

Aims and objectives

- To make and continue a repeating pattern.

Resources

- Template of a blank T-shirt (see below)
- Coloured pencils, crayons, paints or strips of coloured paper to cut out and glue on

Preparation

- Select a range of pirate pictures that show their tops.

What to do

- Look through the pictures and discuss the pirates' tops. Ask, 'What do you notice?' Help the children to identify that they are often striped, with two alternating colours.
- Ask the children if they would like to design their own pirate's shirt.
- On an affirmative response provide the children with a blank T-shirt template and media to use.

- While the children are drawing and colouring talk to them about the *repeating pattern* in the T-shirt. For example, 'What colour are you going to use next? Why that colour? What colour will be on the fifth row? How do you know that?'.

Once the children have selected the (normally two) colours they are going to use, put the others out of reach so they are not tempted to include other colours not originally intended to be in the repeating pattern.

Variations

- Some children may like to design T-shirts that are still patterned but are not made only with stripes!
- The children may be encouraged to bring in an old T-shirt to paint with fabric paints after they have designed their T-shirts. They may wear them if they have a dress-up pirate day or when they are in the role-play pirate ship.

How is this maths?

Mathematics is full of pattern. Seeing pattern helps children to solve problems. Being able to say what comes next helps children to visualise shape or colour and pattern. Using ordinal language (first, second, etc.) helps them to talk mathematically.

Chapter 13
Big and small

Introduction

Thinking about size is a precursor to learning about all aspects of measurement. Children are often very excited to find and make very large items or very small items. Shining an overhead projector onto a big sheet of paper on the wall will provide large images that the children can create their own picture.

Order! Order!

Ordering from smallest to biggest using a range of objects.

Aims and objectives

- To order according to size.

Resources

- A range of objects, either arbitrary objects from the setting/school or items related to a specific topic

Preparation

- None required.

What to do

- Have the items set out on a table and encourage the children to look at them.
- Encourage discussion about what the children see, the attributes of the objects and what they know about them.
- Ask, 'Which object is the *biggest*? How do you know that? Which is the *smallest*? Why do you think that?'
- Take the two objects identified as biggest and smallest and place them at either end of the table. Challenge the children to complete the line, *ordering* the objects from smallest to biggest.
- While the children are doing that, talk to them about the decisions they have made. Ask, 'How do you know this one is bigger than that?'

Carefully select the resources you use to represent 'big' items. A toy elephant that is smaller than a toy mouse may be confusing!

Variation

What exactly is meant by big and small? Order objects in other ways such as *height*, *width*, *weight* and *capacity*. Provide resources for the children to enable them to check their *estimations*.

How is this maths?

This gives children the opportunity to compare different objects. Indirect comparison occurs when children know that if object A is smaller than object B, and object B is smaller than object C, then object A must be smaller than object C. The term for this was coined by Piaget: *transitivity*. It underpins a lot of *logical reasoning* in mathematics.

Making things bigger

Using a magnifying glass or microscope creates lots of possibilities.

Aims and objectives

- To use magnification.
- To find patterns.

Resources

- Small objects that have been collected arbitrarily or that relate to the current topic or theme
- Magnifying glasses
- Microscope (optional)

Preparation

- Create a display of the objects that have been collected.

What to do

- Talk together about the objects. Ask, 'Which object do you like? Why is that?'
- Use a magnifying glass to look at the objects. Talk about what effect the magnifying glass has on the object when they look through it.
- Ask, 'What can you see?' Encourage the children to describe the patterns they can see through the magnifying glass.

Use the magnifying glasses to look at the objects that have been found in the 'Texture' walk (see page 156). Look at how the surface of the objects creates the different textures that were found.

Variation

Use a photocopier or scanner to make things bigger.

How is this maths?

This activity encourages children to think about pattern that occurs naturally. Naturally occurring patterns were a source of interest for mathematicians a long time ago and still fascinate mathematicians and scientists today.

Investigating small creatures

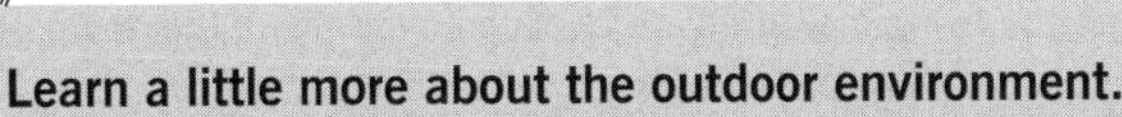

Aims and objectives

- To practise problem solving.
- To look for pattern.

Resources

- An outdoor area that is rich in insects or other wildlife
- Insect observation packs (with clear container and magnifying glass)
- Books on wildlife or pictures of the wildlife in your outdoor area
- Digital camera that takes pictures using the macro setting (optional)
- Paper and pencils for making sketches of the insects

Preparation

- Visit the outdoor area to investigate the possible creatures that you will find. If necessary encourage some creatures, such as woodlice that can be encouraged by laying damp wood flat onto the ground where it is shadier.

What to do

- Explain to the children that they are going to be explorers.
- Share out the equipment the children will be taking exploring with them and discuss what the items are for.
- Talk about being respectful of living things.
- When outside, place the insects or other bugs into the magnifying container one at a time.
- Encourage the children to observe the insect carefully, counting its legs and identifying the three sections to its body (head, thorax and abdomen).
- Ask an adult to take a photograph or the children to sketch the insect.
- Make a note of where it was found and what its habitat is like.

Tips

- **A useful book is Usborne's *1001 Bugs to Spot* by Emma Helbrough and Teri Gower.**
- **Ensure the living creatures are replaced carefully in their own habitat when observations are complete.**

Variation

You could go further afield to visit a bird sanctuary or butterfly house.

How is this maths?

There are many patterns on insects that are mathematical in nature. For example, butterflies and ladybirds have symmetrical patternation. Insects always have six legs: three on the left and three on the right. Similarly spiders have four and four, making eight.

Making a home for wildlife

Encourage more wildlife into the outdoor area.

Aims and objectives

- To practise measuring.
- To learn about categorising.

Resources

- Materials for making the wildlife shelter or home

Preparation

- Research the possible wildlife homes or shelters that are appropriate for your outdoor environment. Gather together the resources required to make the home or shelter. If possible, involve the children in the decision-making.

What to do

- Build the home or shelter together with the children. They will be involved in measuring, cutting, gluing, hammering and so on.
- Once the item has been established, observe the wildlife that uses it (e.g. birds on a feeding station).
- If possible, photograph the visitors and keep a record.
- Display the findings.

Tip Although it is American, the National Wildlife Federation provides a useful checklist for how to create a wildlife habitat that is applicable to all nurseries and schools (www.nwf.org/Get-Outside/Outdoor-Activities/Garden-for-Wildlife/Create-a-Habitat.aspx).

Variation

It may be possible to set up a remote camera inside the home or shelter and observe the wildlife that uses it on the nursery or school computer.

How is this maths?

Making the home or shelter involves *measuring*, which will become more accurate as the children learn more about length. Once the home or shelter is *in situ*, observing the wildlife provides an opportunity for the children to undertake *data handling* or observe *patterns* in the animals' behaviour.

Create something big!

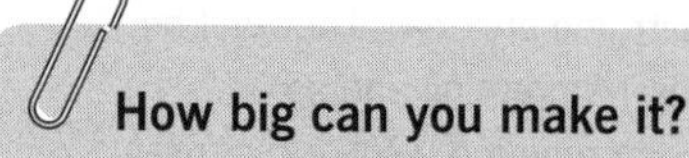

How big can you make it?

Aims and objectives

- To talk about the big, bigger and biggest.

Resources

- Junk modelling materials, including items that are large to the children

Preparation

- Ensure you have gathered enough materials for the children to carry out this activity.

What to do

- Ask the children, 'What is the *biggest* thing you know?' as a way in to discussing very large objects.
- Ask the children if they would like to make the biggest thing they can possibly make.
- Clear a space, indoors or out, that enables the children to start construction.
- Ask, 'Is it *big* enough yet? How can you make it *bigger*? What is the *biggest* you can make?'
- Continue until the children cannot safely make it bigger.

Tips

- ***Bigger*** **relates to a number of physical features of objects, so ensure you provide experiences that include considering** ***height*****,** ***width*** **and** ***weight*****.**
- **Remember to photograph the construction once finished as it will probably have to be dismantled soon after, unless you have a huge area going spare! The children will enjoy dismantling the construction and this will give you an opportunity to talk about** ***small*****,** ***smaller*** **and** ***smallest*****.**

Variation

Instead of using junk materials, can the children make the tallest tower out of construction materials? The children could use papier mâché to make the construction more permanent.

How is this maths?

Exploring size in this way helps children further to understand shape and space. They may also develop their understanding of *infinity*, where space is limitless.

Chapter 14
Jack and the Beanstalk

Introduction

An old favourite, the story of Jack and the Beanstalk offers a number of mathematical activities for young children. Some of the activities in this chapter need a longer time, such as growing seeds, but others can be carried out more quickly. Some of the activities encourage children to visualise height and distance; creating and manipulating pictures in the mind helps children's mathematical thinking as they move through primary school and beyond.

Planting seeds

Observe Jack's beans grow.

Aims and objectives

- To learn about measuring.
- To practise ordering.

Resources

- Bean seeds (any climbing variety)
- Clear containers for planting (some yoghurt pots are clear enough and can be recycled for this purpose)
- Cotton wool or compost
- Digital camera (optional)

Preparation

- Ensure there is a space in the nursery or classroom for the bean pots to be observed easily.

What to do

- Plant the climbing bean seeds in the clear containers. Ensure that the bean seed is pressed against the side of the container if you want the children to observe the root growth.
- Keep the seeds watered well.
- Observe the plant growth every day. If possible, photograph the bean daily to keep a record of the growth.
- Display the photos to show the development.
- Photos should be ordered appropriately.

Tip Other plants that grow quickly are peas and sunflowers.

Variations

- The children may also measure the *length* of the bean plant as it grows, writing the length in *centimetres* in a table or chart.
- Photographs can also be used to record other changes, such as shadows over a day.

How is this maths?

Change over time can be recorded, either by photograph or by other data (such as measures). Understanding this starts children on the road of recording scientific evidence and understanding data handling.

Let's harp on about it

Make a harp to serenade the golden goose and encourage her to lay some golden eggs.

Aims and objectives

- To learn about length and pitch.

Resources

- Elastic bands
- Wood
- Nails
- Hammer

Preparation

- None required.

What to do

- Hammer into the wood a series of nails along the base. Hammer in above corresponding nails so that the distance between the base nail and the nail above it increases each time (see illustration).
- Stretch the elastic bands between each base nail and the nail above it.
- Play the 'harp', listening to how the sound changes depending on the length of each elastic band.
- Talk about why the sounds change.

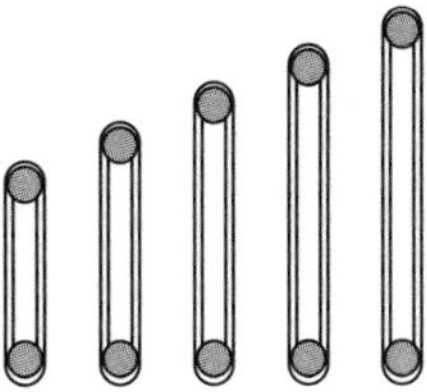

Tip **The pitch becomes higher as the elastic band is stretched further.**

Variation

Instead of using wood and nails, stretch the elastic bands over a variety of different-sized plastic containers.

How is this maths?

Pitch and harmonics are closely related to *fractions*. This is an early way to explore this concept.

Golden eggs

Help the giant and Jack keep account of the golden eggs.

Aims and objectives

- To practise addition.
- To practise subtraction.

Resources

- Golden eggs (these could be boiled eggs that have been spray-painted, golden-wrapped Easter eggs or plastic toy eggs)
- A basket

Preparation

- If possible, reread the story of 'Jack and the Beanstalk' and focus discussion around the goose laying the golden eggs and Jack stealing them.

What to do

- Count three eggs into the basket, saying that the goose has laid these eggs for the giant.
- Tell the children that Jack *takes two* of the eggs and count two eggs as they are taken out.
- Ask the children, 'How many eggs are in the giant's basket now?' Encourage the children to explain why they think there is that number of eggs left. Check.
- Continue the activity by placing eggs into the basket and removing some.

- **Ask the children to suggest the number of eggs that the goose lays or Jack steals. This would help you to assess their understanding of number in this context.**
- **Vary the number of eggs used depending on the children's attainment.**

Variation

You could use an egg carton to hold the eggs instead of a basket. This would help the children to visualise the numbers in a context that may be more familiar to them.

How is this maths?

The children are *counting*, *adding* and *taking away* the eggs. They are *visualising* the number of eggs in the basket and checking their *mental calculations*.

Retelling Jack and the Beanstalk

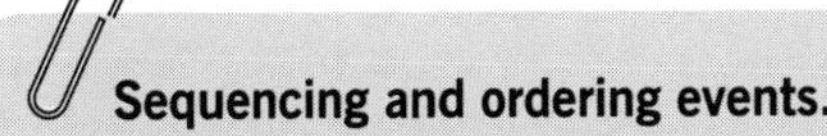

Aims and objectives

- To learn about sequencing.
- To learn about ordering.

Resources

- The 'Jack and the Beanstalk' story
- Either a template with spaces for the children to draw pictures or write about the key events in the story, or pictures from the book of key events that the children can put into order
- Prompt cards of ordinal and time-related words for display as a memory aid (optional)

Preparation

- None required.

What to do

- Read (or reread) the 'Jack and the Beanstalk' story.
- Talk together about what happened *first* in the story. Ask, 'What happened *next*?' and so on until the story has been retold.
- Ask the children to work in pairs to retell the story to each other. Encourage them to use language such as *first*, *second*, *third*, *next*, *then* and *last*. If available and appropriate, display these words as an *aide-mémoire* for the children.
- After retelling to each other, give out the templates or the story pictures and ask the children to record their story to show the correct order.

For younger children use the pictures in the book to support the retelling of the story.

Variations

- The children can act out the story in small groups instead of recording it as above.
- Any stories can be recalled and ordinal and time-related language encouraged.

How is this maths?

Some mathematical tasks require children to find the solution by carrying out a series of steps in a particular *order*. This activity helps children to think about sequence. The activity also helps children to use *ordinal language* such as *first*, *second* and *third* as well as *time*-related vocabulary such as *next*, *then* and *last*.

Climb the beanstalk

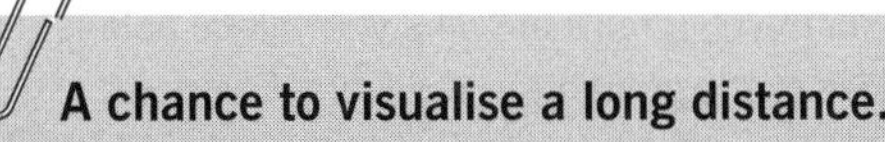

A chance to visualise a long distance.

Aims and objectives

- To visualise length and distance.

Resources

- None required

Preparation

- If possible, reread the story of 'Jack and the Beanstalk' and focus discussion around Jack climbing up and down the beanstalk.

What to do

- Ask the children to pretend to be Jack climbing the beanstalk.
- Wave goodbye to Mum and start climbing the imaginary stalk. As you start, look at the house behind Mum. Ask, 'What size is it?' (big).
- After a short time ask who is getting tired. Show the children that you are tired. Perhaps wipe your brow with one arm but then hold onto the beanstalk again quickly for fear of falling. Explain your arms are aching and your legs are tired.
- Talk with the children about how you have all climbed a long, long way up the beanstalk and that you are nearly at the giant's house.
- Ask, 'What was that noise?' Explain you heard the giant and you all need to get home. Look down. 'Can you see your house? How big is it from all the way up here?' (It is very very small, almost so small it cannot be seen!)
- Climb down the beanstalk. Look down again. 'What can you see now?' 'How big is your house now?' (Encourage the children to think of an item that is about the same size, for example a mouse.)

- As you climb further down the imaginary beanstalk continue to ask the children to look down and explain how big their house looks now. Depending on the children's answers you will be able to comment on how close to the ground they now are. Compare different children's responses with each other by commenting that one child must have climbed down faster than another.

Tip If you have another adult they may shout 'Fee-fi-fo-fum' at the appropriate time to initiate the descent.

Variation

You could also look up as you climb or descend to visualise or imagine the giant's castle.

How is this maths?

The children will be exploring *perspective* through imagining climbing and descending the beanstalk. They will visualise *distance* and the impact that this has on objects that are a long way away. Artists often use mathematics to develop perspective in their pictures. Perspective mathematics is also used to design the spray-painted advertisements on sports pitches that look as if they are standing up, creating a clever illusion.

One small step for Jack, one giant step outside!

Think about the giant by investigating his footprint.

Aims and objectives

- To practise visualisation of size.
- To practise measuring.

Resources

- Mud, sand or similar for creating the giant's footprint
- Letter from the giant (see wording below)
- Template of footprint if needed

Preparation

- Before the children arrive, set up the giant's footprint outside using appropriate resources. Try to make the footprint as large as it can possibly be.
- Prepare another adult for their role.

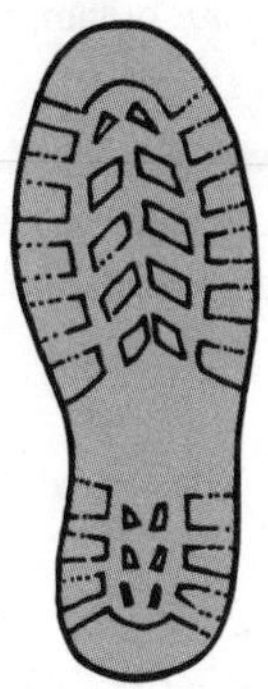

What to do

- At a prearranged time send another adult outside for some reason while you are doing something else with the children.

- On their return the other adult will be excited because they think that the giant may have been around the nursery/school looking for Jack because he has left a muddy footprint outside!
- Take the children outside to look at the evidence. Talk about the footprint: 'How *long* is the footprint?' *Measure* it if appropriate. 'How *wide* is the footprint? So how big do you think the giant's foot actually is? Show me how long a toe might be!'
- Ask the children to wonder how *tall* the giant might be if this is his footprint. Encourage them to visualise the giant's *height* by comparing it to the nursery/school buildings.

Tips

- **If you are not confident in producing the footprint from scratch yourself, use an overhead projector to shine a shoe print onto a large sheet of card. Use this as your template.**
- **If you think any children will become distressed at the thought of a giant coming into the premises then avoid this activity. Alternatively you or another adult could find a letter from the giant that reads:**

  Dear children

  I have been looking for Jack because I know he has been stealing my golden eggs. I'm afraid that I left a rather muddy footprint in your playground and because your broom was too small for me to use I had to leave it there!

  I know that Jack is not with you and so I will not visit any of you again. I am sorry to disturb you. I'd also like you to know that I really am a friendly giant and very polite, not like the story tells you!

  Kind regards

  The Giant

Variations

- Use chalk on the carpet inside – keep the proportion of the footprint so that the giant could fit in the room!
- The children may write back to the giant telling him what they have investigated and know about his height, toe-size and foot-length, etc.

How is this maths?

The children are exploring very early ideas of *ratio* and *proportion* by using the foot to visualise the height of the giant.

Chapter 15
Towers

Introduction

This chapter is very much related to length and height. If you are near a building that contains a number of stairs you may want to take the children on a walk to climb them, counting how many steps they have climbed. Thinking about different towers within the children's environment and beyond helps them to understand construction further, which later develops into geometric understanding.

Tall tower competition

Whose tower is the tallest?

Aims and objectives

- To learn about indirect comparison of length.

Resources

- Construction equipment
- Masking tape
- Unmarked stick

Preparation

- Use the masking tape to identify the areas within which the children must construct their towers, ensuring that the spaces are as far away from each other as possible.

What to do

- Announce that there is a competition to build the tallest tower using the materials in the construction area.
- Show the children the area that their group will be constructing the tower within.
- Announce the time they have and set them off on the task.
- During construction speak to the children about how they are constructing their towers and how they plan to make them *tall*, or the *tallest*.
- At the end of construction talk about which tower is the *tallest*. How can the children check without moving their towers?
- Using the unmarked stick, place it next to each tower in turn and mark the height of each. Use this to check the tallest tower.
- You may wish to award a small prize to the winning team!

Tip

Provide a lot of equipment. You may need to borrow equipment from other classrooms. If so, identify it in some way so it can be returned safely.

Variations

- Have only one group at a time building a tower and use the stick to record the heights. Challenge the next group to build their tower higher. Keep going until all groups have had a turn.
- Alternatively build one tower that each group contributes to.

How is this maths?

The children are exploring length and what terms such as *longer* mean. By using the stick they are using *indirect comparison* to identify the tallest tower. Indirect comparison occurs when children know that if tower A is taller than tower B, and tower B is taller than tower C, then tower A must be taller than tower C. The term for this was coined by Piaget: *transitivity*. It underpins a lot of logical reasoning in mathematics.

Construct a tall tower

A less competitive version of the previous activity.

Aims and objectives

- To practise direct comparison of length.

Resources

- Wooden blocks of various shapes
- Pictures of world-famous towers such as Eiffel Tower (Paris), Freedom Tower (Miami), Qutub Minar Tower (Delhi) and Emirates Tower (Dubai).

Preparation

- Study the pictures of the famous towers from around the world.

What to do

- Challenge a small group to build a tower that is taller than one of the children in the group.
- As they are building it, speak to them about their design and how they are ensuring that it will not fall down. Explore what shapes they are using to ensure the tower is as secure as possible, drawing on what they saw in the pictures of other towers.

Tip **A tower may be more secure if it is wider at the bottom and narrower at the top.**

Variations

- Use different construction materials.
- Build other objects rather than towers.

How is this maths?

The children are developing and using their knowledge of shape and space to build a tower that is *taller* than them. They will use *trial and error* throughout. Learning from mistakes is an important skill when developing a mathematical disposition.

Drawing a tower

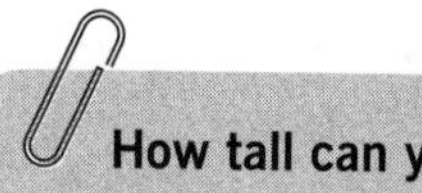

How tall can you go?

Aims and objectives

- To explore the relationship between length and height.

Resources

- Long thin paper
- Pencils

Preparation

- Show the children the pictures of the towers you have gathered together for 'Construct a tall tower' to encourage them to think about what towers look like.

What to do

- Have a selection of paper of different lengths for the children to choose from.
- Encourage the children to draw their tower on the paper. Discuss with them how *long* and *wide* it is.
- When the towers are finished display them on a wall. Discuss the *heights* of the towers and *order* them. Did the towers look different when they were flat on the table? Have they really changed, or do they look the same?

Allow the children to change the dimension that they are working in. For example, do they want to work on the floor or on the paper stapled to the wall? Encourage them to hold the paper up in different directions.

Variation

This is not limited to drawing towers. The children can draw people or giraffes, flowers or trees, or shapes, or write numbers on a long strip of paper.

How is this maths?

Young children find it difficult to understand that an object does not change when it has moved from the horizontal plane to the vertical plane and vice versa. Enabling them to manipulate their own drawings and paper allows them to explore *conservation of length*.

Thinking about towers

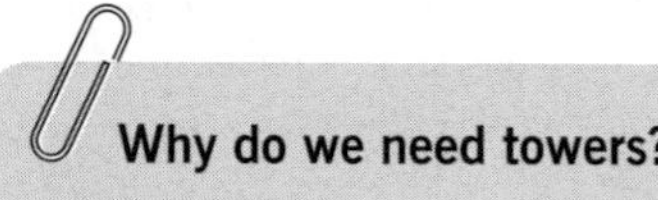

Why do we need towers?

Aims and objectives

- To understand the use and application of tall structures.

Resources

- A set of photographs of towers in the local area or from further afield

Preparation

- Take photos of towers in the local vicinity to add to the other tower pictures the children have been using.

What to do

- Talk to the children about the towers that they are familiar with in their environment. Find the tower(s) they are talking about from the picture bank to help the other children engage in discussion.
- Show other towers. Ask, 'What are the towers used for?'
- Once individual towers have been discussed, encourage the children to identify common features of some of the towers. For example, accommodation and office blocks enable a lot of people to live and work in an area that is very limited on the ground. Some towers (pylons) are designed to keep items (cables) safely off the ground and away from people, and other towers (mobile phone masts or aircraft control towers) have to lift something permanently (signals or controllers) high into the sky.

This activity helps children to think about towers being used for a number of different purposes and challenges their stereotypical notions of what towers are for (e.g. Rapunzel).

Variation

Include talk about historical towers such as lighthouses and television signal transmitters.

How is this maths?

As well as knowing mathematical facts, children also need to know how mathematical concepts are used and applied in real life. This helps make mathematics meaningful to them and shows how mathematics has a purpose.

Being tall

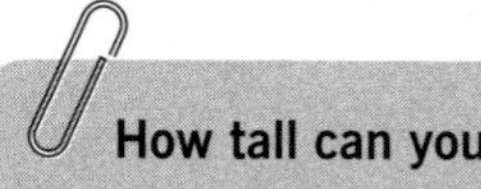

How tall can you be?

Aims and objectives

- To make ourselves tall, taller and tallest.

Resources

- None required

Preparation

- None required.

What to do

- Ask the children, 'Can you stretch like a tower? Show me.'
- Ask the children to move around the room like tall animals they know, such as a giraffe, llama or elephant.
- Ask, 'Why do these animals need to be tall?'.

Tip **These animals are taller than us, but they all move differently. Some creatures have developed wings so they can fly to reach food sources and also to be protected.**

Variation

The children can also move like animals to explore other notions such as speed or agility.

How is this maths?

The children are exploring the notion of height. Understanding concepts related to *measures*, *shape* and *space* will help develop more sophisticated geometric thinking later.

Lock her in the tower!

Use animated film to explore and visualise spirals and height.

Aims and objectives

- To link shape and height.

Resources

- A clip of an animated film where a fair maiden, princess or similar has been kept captive in a tower

Preparation

- None required.

What to do

- Play the video clip.
- Discuss, 'Why do you think the girl was locked in a tower?' (For inaccessibility reasons.)
- 'How is it possible to get into the room at top of the tower?' (Via a spiral staircase.)
- 'Why a spiral staircase?' (Because the stairs would be too steep if it was not curved.)
- 'What other ways could the girl escape?'

Tip **Show other video clips to help contrast with the first one played.**

Variation

Be as creative as possible in developing escape routes. Which ones would be most effective? Why?

How is this maths?

The children are visualising a *spiral* inside a *cone*-shaped tower. Mathematically speaking, if the tower is not tapered towards the top and it is *cylindrical* the staircase is technically a *helix*, but don't be too picky about that! Understanding concepts related to *measures*, *shape* and *space* will help develop more sophisticated geometric thinking later.

Chapter 16
The café

Introduction

The activities in this chapter could be carried out in a larger space, such as a school hall, or outside area, or in a café set up in the role-play area. They could also be carried out by all the children together, taking on different roles such as the waiting staff, the kitchen staff or the customers. Alternatively children might prefer to take turns. You may have a local café that the children can tour before they are involved in setting up their café in the nursery or school. Parents or children from another class might be invited to the café also.

The tables

Transform the room into a café.

Aims and objectives

- To practise 1-to-1 correspondence.
- To count in twos or fives.

Resources

- Classroom tables
- Table numbers for display
- Chairs

Preparation

- Arrange the tables into a café style, perhaps with a small group of children helping. Discuss with the children how they would like the tables be set out.

What to do

- Arrange the tables so the children are sitting in twos or fives – practise counting in twos or fives together so see how many people are in the café.
- Place a table number on each table, to help with ordering and taking orders (see later activities).
- What will be at each setting? Spoons, place mats, serviettes? Once decisions have been made, encourage the children to set their own place at the table.

Tip

Take a trip to a local café to look at how the tables are arranged, as well as the other activities that go on there.

Variation

Setting the table can also happen in the doll's house, at a restaurant, at home in the role-play area or at lunchtime in the dining room/dining area.

How is this maths?

It is important that children understand *1-to-1 correspondence*, identifying a relationship between two or more items. For example, in this activity the children will know that for each child there should be one knife, one fork, one spoon and one tumbler. Later on in mathematics relationships beyond 1-to-1 develop. These are used to solve problems, undertake statistical analyses, algebra and many other tasks.

Garçon, I'd like to order please

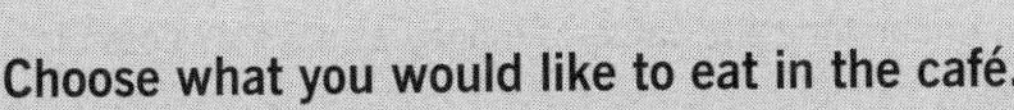

Choose what you would like to eat in the café.

Aims and objectives

- To recognise and read numbers in a money context.

Resources

- Café menus
- Coins (toy or real)

Preparation

- The menus may have been created by the children earlier.
- Give the children coins to spend in the café.

What to do

- In pairs children look at the menus and the *price* of the items available. They talk about what they would like. They discuss the price of the food and how much *money* they have to spend.

Tip **Discuss the menus with the children first, if they have not been involved in making them. Use pictures of the food items to support their comprehension. Also show the number of *coins* required alongside the value in numbers.**

Variations

Ordering food and paying for it can happen in a wide range of contexts and the role-play area provides the ideal opportunity for this. For example, it could turn into a fish and chip shop, a Chinese takeaway, an Indian restaurant, a baker's shop, a pâtisserie, a pie shop or a butcher's shop.

How is this maths?

Children need to recognise and name coins. As we move towards living in a cashless society where everything is paid by card or other means, it is essential that young children understand the value of money as soon as possible.

May I take your order now?

A follow-on activity in the café.

Aims and objectives

- To write numbers.

Resources

- Notepads and pencils
- Dressing-up clothes for each *garçon* (waiter) and *serveuse* (waitress)

Preparation

- None required, if previous two activities have been undertaken.

What to do

- Explain to the waiters and waitresses their role, which includes:
  a. Writing the table number down
  b. Taking the order
  c. Leaving the bill
  d. Collecting the money
- With adult assistance, send the waiters and waitresses to their customers!

If you number each item on the menu the waiters and waitresses can write the relevant number rather than needing to write the item's name.

Variations

- Orders can be taken in any of the places listed earlier, i.e. the role-play fish and chip shop, Chinese takeaway, Indian restaurant, baker's shop, pâtisserie, pie shop or butcher's shop.
- Orders could be taken on the telephone in these places and the customer could find their items waiting to be collected when they arrive at the role play area.

How is this maths?

The children are using mathematics to record information. For example, they are writing table numbers and menu items or their corresponding numbers. Using and applying their mathematical knowledge is an important skill to encourage and develop.

Mixing drinks

Make yummy fruit squash to drink in the café.

Aims and objectives

- To practise counting.
- To use ratio.
- To learn about capacity.

Resources

- Fruit squash concentrate
- Jugs
- Cups or tumblers
- Drinking water

Preparation

- Check children's health records regarding allergies to ensure all children are able to partake.

What to do

- The drinks need to be made up to pass on to the customers.
- Read the label of the squash together. What does it mean 'to *every part* concentrate add six parts water'?
- Discuss, 'How much does this jug hold?'. Encourage the children to count the number of cups that go into the jug. Start with one 'part' concentrate. Count it into the jug together. Add six 'parts' water. Discuss whether or not the children think there is room for another seven cups to be added. Add more if so. Keep going until the jug is full.
- When ready pour the squash into cups. Ask, 'How many drinks have we made? Is that enough? How many more do we need? How do we know where to fill the jug to?'

Think carefully about what will measure the 'part'. It doesn't have to be a cup, it could be any clean item. Try to select something small enough to require the children to undertake the activity more than once.

Variation

Follow recipes for fruit cocktails. For example, an 'orange and lemon zest' could contain five parts orange juice, one part lemon juice and three parts lemonade.

How is this maths?

The children are using *ratio* to make the squash. In the example above the ratio is one part concentrate to six parts water. That is a ratio of 1:6. Engaging in activities that require children to use ratios in meaningful situations early on helps children to be able to calculate using ratios, and learn the relationship between ratio and proportion, fractions, percentages and decimals, later in their primary school career.

I choose that glass

Glass sizes can be deceptive!

Aims and objectives

- To understand conservation of capacity.
- To check the accuracy of results.

Resources

- A range of tumblers (approximately six) that hold a varying amount of liquid

Preparation

- Ensure two or three of the tumblers hold less than they look like they might, compared with the other tumblers.

What to do

- Tell the children that they can choose any tumbler they wish to have their favourite drink in.
- Discuss which one(s) they would choose and why.

- Focus on the decision made by some children to select the tumbler that holds the most. Ask, 'How do you know that tumbler holds the *most*? How would we *check*?' (Do not check at this stage.)
- Ask the children to see if they can *order* the tumblers from the one that holds the *most* to the one that holds the *least*.
- During their discussions if necessary challenge their thinking. For example, if they are focusing only on height point out to them that the tall tumbler is very thin but another (shorter) tumbler is wider.
- Once they have made their decision ask them how they may check to see if they have got the order correct.
- The children check using their own method. If there were some mistakes encourage the children to discuss why they were wrong.

Tip Some children may choose a tumbler because it is attractive to them, rather than because it is the largest. This is fine. However, focus on the response of a child who chooses the largest tumbler.

Variation

Bottles can also be used to explore *conservation of capacity*. Parcels that are different sizes and weights (i.e. some small heavy parcels and one or two larger light ones) can also be used to explore *conservation of weight*.

How is this maths?

Conservation of capacity is a difficult concept for children to understand because the visual impact that the object has means that we often focus on the height only, rather than its capacity. By having many opportunities to explore conservation of capacity, experience will help children to develop their understanding.

Decorating biscuits

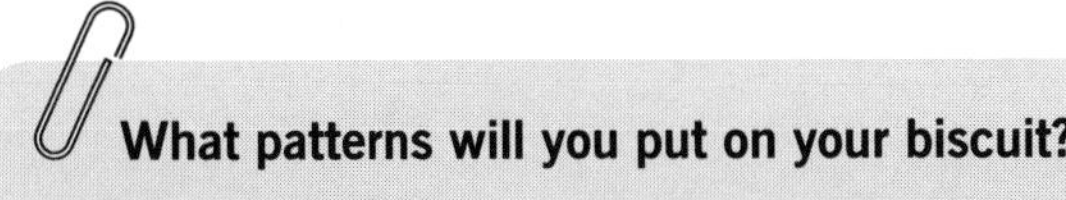

Aims and objectives

- To make and continue a pattern.

Resources

- Biscuits
- White icing
- Icing pens
- Sweets
- Sprinkles

Preparation

- The biscuits may have been made earlier by the children or could be shop-bought.

What to do

- Spread the biscuits with the white icing.
- Use sweets, sprinkles or icing pens to create a design.

Provide a range of biscuit shapes. Circular biscuits encourage symmetrical patterns with more lines of symmetry than rectangular biscuits.

Variation

Ice the biscuits according to a theme, or make your own biscuits so the children have a wider range of shapes to decorate, such as stars.

How is this maths?

Mathematics is full of *pattern* in number and shape. Seeing pattern helps children to solve problems. Being able to say what comes next helps children to visualise shape or colour and pattern. Using *ordinal language* (first, second, etc.) helps children to talk mathematically.

Displaying the biscuits

How are we going to 'show off' the biscuits for premium sales?

Aims and objectives

- To understand pattern.

Resources

- Cake platters – a selection
- Digital camera (optional)

Preparation

- None required.

What to do

- Ask the children how the biscuits can be displayed for the most sales.
- The children might arrange them on a tiered cake stand. If so, is there logic to their presentation? (Either in the numbers placed on each tier, or placing like biscuits together, or alternating the biscuits, etc.)
- The children might take photos of the biscuits and display those.

Allow the children to decide themselves and their creativity may surprise you!

Variation

Hang the biscuits from the Christmas tree.

How is this maths?

The children are creating their own *patterns* using the biscuits. They are using their *logical thinking* to do this. Pattern and logic are both essential skills for children to develop in mathematics as they support children in carrying out mathematical tasks later on.

Chapter 17
Fun with numbers

Introduction

The activities in this chapter are focused on children learning about numbers. They will explore numbers in a wide range of contexts and see numbers displayed in many different ways. Encourage the children to think about large numbers also – they get very excited by looking at and reading numbers such as 100 or 1000!

Air finger-numbers

Create numbers using only your index finger.

Aims and objectives

- To read and write numbers.

Resources

- None required

Preparation

- None required.

What to do

- The children trace numbers in the air with their index finger, using big movements.

Children love to write numbers that are related to them, such as their age, how old they will be next birthday, their house number and so on.

Variation

The children hold a short stick that has a ribbon attached to it and make numbers in the air with the tip of the stick.

How is this maths?

The children are learning to write numerals.

Other numbers at your fingertips

Make numbers with your finger using a range of materials.

Aims and objectives

- To read and write numbers.

Resources

- Paint
- Shaving foam
- Sand
- Trays

Preparation

- Pour each of the resources into their own tray. The paint needs to be a very thin layer.

What to do

- Write numbers in the shaving foam, paint or sand.
- Encourage the children to follow your lead.
- Ask them to write certain numbers or ask them what numbers they want to write.
- Use a flat hand to rebuild the shaving foam or shake the trays of paint or sand to start again.

Tips

- The shaving foam offers a slightly different texture for the children to explore.
- As well as creating the numbers ask the children what they know about the number – for example, is it their age? Mummy's age? What number does it come after? What is the number after that?

Variations

- Glue and glitter or PVA and string/wool offer another texture to write in.
- Try breathing on a mirrored surface and writing with a finger in the condensation.

How is this maths?

The children are learning to write numerals.

Play dough numbers

Make lots of snakes and turn them into numbers.

Aims and objectives

- To read and write numbers.

Resources

- Play dough

Preparation

- If necessary, make the play dough. Here is a recipe if you do not have one already:

  250g plain flour, 50g salt, 140ml water, 1–2 tablespoons of cooking oil and, if using, a few drops of food colouring.

  Mix the flour and salt in a large bowl. Add the water and oil. Knead well (add slightly more flour or water as necessary) until the dough is smooth and not sticky. Add food colouring and continue to knead until the colour is fully blended. Place into a plastic bag and refrigerate until chilled.

What to do

- With the children roll the play dough into 'snakes' (long and skinny sausage shapes).
- Use the 'snakes' to form numbers they are familiar with.
- Can the group make all the numbers from one to ten?
- Can the digits be used to make other numbers the children know?
- What is the biggest number they know?

Identify a number that the children are still learning and ask them to make small and big play dough versions of the same number. This will help to consolidate what the number looks like because they are repeating it several times.

Variation

The children could make their names out of play dough letters.

How is this maths?

The children are learning to read and construct numerals.

String-thing numbers

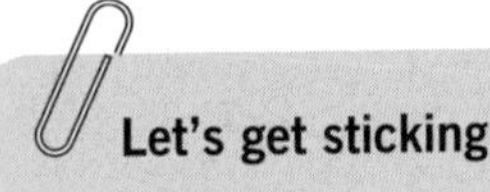

Let's get sticking!

Aims and objectives

- To read and write numbers.

Resources

- Glue stick or craft glue
- Wool or string
- Card or thick paper

Preparation

- None required.

What to do

- Encourage the children to 'draw' a number using the glue.
- Cover the glue with wool or string.
- Display.

Tip

During the task talk with the children about what they know about their numbers. 'How is the number made? Where do you see the number? What numbers is it *between* when you count? Name a number *greater than* that number. Name a number *less than* that number.'

Variation

Use glue and then sprinkle glitter over to make the numbers.

How is this maths?

The children are learning to read and construct numerals. They are also sharing with their peers and adults what they know about numbers.

Making big numbers

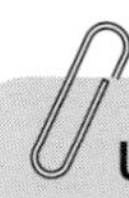

Use whole bodies to make numbers.

Aims and objectives

- To read and write numbers.

Resources

- Large floor space such as a hall
- A4 sheets with the numbers 1–10 on them

Preparation

- None required.

What to do

- Ask a small group of children to lie on the floor while their peers shape them into a number.
- Repeat for many numbers. Talk about which numbers are similar in shape and why.

Tip **Take a photo looking down on the children so the participants can see the outcome also.**

Variation

Use larger numbers or ask children to create their own numbers within their group so more children have an opportunity to join in each time.

How is this maths?

This activity helps children to identify where numbers are similar and different, which can help them talk about common errors made such as reversing their 5s, or confusing 2 and 5 with each other.

'I can' with a calculator

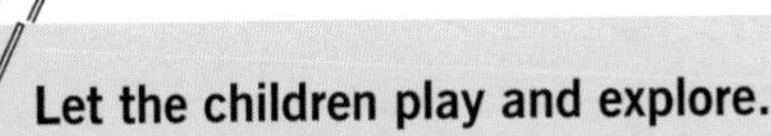

Let the children play and explore.

Aims and objectives

- To read and write numbers.

Resources

- Calculators

Preparation

- None required.

What to do

- Provide the children with calculators to explore what numbers they can make.
- Read the numbers they create for them if they are unable to.
- Ask them to challenge each other to make numbers.

Tip The children will enjoy listening to you read off the calculator numbers they have never heard before, such as twenty-three million, four hundred and sixty-four thousand, one hundred and seventy-six!

Variation

Give no direction and let the children have free access to the calculators over a period of time. After a designated period ask them to share with each other what they have found out.

How is this maths?

The children will explore numbers that are far larger than those that regular nursery or setting activities might offer. It also introduces *decimal* and *negative* numbers to the children. This activity excites young children who want to find out more about these new numbers!

Numbers we use

We use numbers all the time – let's explore!

Aims and objectives

- To read numbers.
- To use and apply number.

Resources

- A number of photographs or pictures of numbers in everyday use (for examples see 'What to do' section)

Preparation

- Take photos if necessary.

What to do

- Share the photographs/pictures.
- Talk with the children about where they have seen the numbers (e.g. house doors, the supermarket, on birthday cards, on dice) and how they are used.
- Talk about the different representations (dice use dots, money has a decimal point in the middle of the number to show the pounds and pence, the road sign is big for people to see how fast they are allowed to travel).
- Encourage the children to bring in their own examples of where they have seen numbers (e.g. the newspaper, a rubbing of their parents' car registration plate).
- Display their numbers alongside yours.

The key to this activity is to get the children talking about their own experiences of number, where they see them and how they use number.

Variation

You could do the same with shapes or with letters of the alphabet.

How is this maths?

This activity helps children to see how numbers support many *purposes* and how they give *order* and *structure*, which makes life easier and safer for us.

Chapter 18
Weather

Introduction

A number of the activities in this chapter make use of any outdoor area available. If your outdoor space is limited then the activities can be adapted accordingly. Looking at weather and seasons across a year helps children to see a large-scale natural pattern. You could talk and sing about the seasons over a short period, or dedicate a small display space for a whole year to photographs of the children and the trees through the seasons to illustrate how they adapt in different types of weather.

Our weather station

Let's explore our local weather ourselves!

Aims and objectives

- To measure using different units.

Resources

- Scissors
- Sticky tape and Blu-Tack® or similar
- Rulers
- Paper
- Pencils
- A sturdy plastic or wooden box that can stand on its side
- White paint
- A thermometer
- A pen top
- Plastic fizzy drink bottles (3)
- Card
- A knitting needle
- Matchsticks
- A cork
- Sand

Preparation

- Announce to the children's parents that the children will be making a weather station.
- Ask for donations of the resources identified above.
- Visit www.metoffice.gov.uk/education/kids/weather_station.html for instructions on making the weather station.

What to do

- Construct a weather station together that:
  a. Collects rainfall (rain gauge)
  b. Measures the temperature (thermometer)
  c. Shows wind direction (wind vane)

Tips

- **Take daily measurements and record these together on a daily, weekly or monthly weather chart.**
- **Instead of making the wind vane that is on the Met Office website it is possible to make a very simple wind 'sock' by attaching thin, light ribbon to the end of a garden cane.**

Variation

You may even want to include a home-made barometer! (Visit www.familyfun.go.com/crafts/balloon-barometer-848821/ for more details.)

How is this maths?

To construct the weather station the children will be *measuring* using *length*. When they start gathering and collecting *data* from the weather station they will also be measuring in other units, such as *temperature* in degrees Celsius and wind direction according to the *compass directions*.

Wind

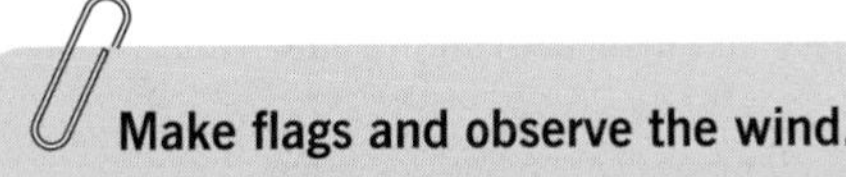

Make flags and observe the wind.

Aims and objectives

- To practise logical thinking.

Resources

- Garden canes or sticks
- Thin fabric
- Glue

Preparation

- Make the flags:
  a. Cut different shapes out of the fabric.
  b. Glue along the end of the fabric that is to be attached to the cane. Press the glued edge to the cane and leave until completely dry.

What to do

- Watch the wind blow the grass and the leaves on the trees.
- Take the flags made previously outside.
- Do they fly differently in different parts of the outdoor area?

Hold the flags at the same height to get a fairer test around the premises.

Variation

Make windmills instead of flags.

How is this maths?

Understanding *cause and effect* makes use of logical thinking. Understanding why the flags fly better in some locations than others utilises this skill.

Shadows

Observe how shadows change during the day.

Aims and objectives

- To notice change.

Resources

- Outdoor area that has the sun all day
- Outdoor chalk
- Large paper and felt-tip pen (optional)

Preparation

- Check the weather forecast to ensure the sun is going to stay out all day.

What to do

- Draw around a child's shadow at different times of the day (e.g. 9am, noon, 3pm).
- Discuss what happens over the day.
- Ask why it happens.

Tip

Remember that the sun is not moving. Rather, it is the earth spinning on its axis that makes the shadows change. Try to avoid suggesting to the children that the sun moves (although they will come up with this misconception themselves because this is what they think they observe).

Variation

If possible draw on large paper and keep. Then redo in winter. How are the shadows different now? Why? Discuss *length* of shadows, the *height* of the sun against the horizon and how the sun appears to travel across the sky during the day.

How is this maths?

The children are talking about how the shadows change in relation to length and also direction (angle). They are beginning to explore Earth and our sun, for which there are many patterns and cycles that have been explained using mathematics.

Create your own shadows

Use a torch or overhead projector to make shadows on the wall.

Aims and objectives

- To learn about movement.
- To learn about shape.

Resources

- Torch or overhead projector
- Blank wall

Preparation

- Move the projector (if using one) into position before the children arrive. Ensure the lead is safely taped down.

What to do

- Encourage the children to make shadows against the wall using an overhead projector or a torch.
  Ask:
  a. '*How many* fingers/toys can you see?'
  b. 'Can you move the shadow *fast/slowly*?'
  c. 'Can you move the shadow *high/low*?'
  d. 'Can you make a *wide* shadow or a *narrow* shadow?'
  e. 'Can the shadow jump *up* and *down*?'
  f. 'What else can your shadow do?'

Let the children play and explore for some time before asking your questions.

Variations

- You may set up a plain, light-coloured sheet with a light source behind it instead.
- The children could use shadow puppets to make them move as per the questions above.

How is this maths?

There are a number of mathematical concepts being explored in this activity, mainly related to shape and space. By forming the shadows the children may have to think on another plane, depending on the position of the light source. Making a wide or narrow shadow may require the child to move in and out from the light source, which also requires them to use a different plane.

The four seasons

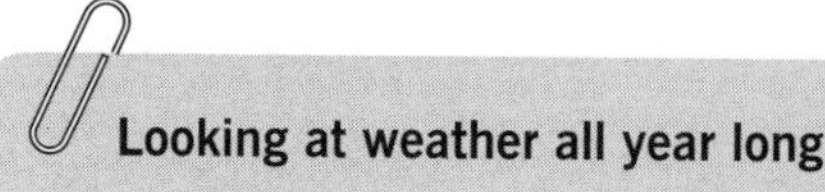

Looking at weather all year long.

Aims and objectives

- To understand repeating patterns.

Change throughout the year

Let's spring into action!

Aims and objectives

- To understand repeating patterns.

Resources

- Brainstorming paper
- Felt-tip pens
- Pictures showing people out and about in each of the seasons (optional)
- *Lili's Wish* by Emma Thomson (optional)

Preparation

- Read *Lili's Wish* by Emma Thomson (optional). This pop-up book follows the story of rag doll Lili who, with her friends' help, works out she is one year old by thinking about key events she remembers happening in each of the seasons.

What to do

- Talk with the children about what they know about each of the four seasons. Ask questions such as:
  a. 'How do the trees change?'
  b. 'What flowers do you see?'
  c. 'What is the weather like?'
  d. 'What clothes do you wear?'

- Record their answers, or ask the children to draw their ideas on the brainstorming sheet.
- Bring the four seasons together. How is the weather in each season different?
- Talk about the cyclical pattern that the seasons make.

Tip **You may look at a different season each day, or split the class into four groups with each group focusing on one season.**

Variations

- Listen to Vivaldi's 'Four Seasons' while you are thinking about the seasons.
- Look at a life cycle presented by month or season (see www.ladybird-survey.org/lifecycle.aspx for one example). Discuss the impact the seasons have on the life cycle.

How is this maths?

Mathematicians look at all sorts of patterns. Some of them repeat after a very short time, others such as the seasons repeat after a much longer time. Understanding that some patterns are cyclical is an important mathematical notion to begin to develop.

Celebrating through the seasons

Taking a look at how the children celebrate their birthdays around the year.

Aims and objectives

- To practise logical reasoning.

Resources

- Photos of children's birthday parties (ask the children to bring these in beforehand)

Preparation

- Request party photographs from parents.
- Check children's birthday dates to confirm in which season they fall.

What to do

- Talk with the children about how they celebrate their birthdays by sharing the photos they have brought in. Ask them not to reveal the date of the birthday!
- Discuss the clothes that the guests are wearing. Ask why the children would be dressed like that.
- Ask the other children to identify which season the party may have been held in.
- Check when the child's birthday is. Were the class correct?

Tip **You may also talk about the location of the party (particularly if it is outdoors in the summer). Be mindful that not all the children will have had similar experiences of birthday parties.**

Variation

You can talk about other celebrations through the year, or take one celebration (e.g. Christmas) and look at how others in Australia or New Zealand celebrate it in a different season.

How is this maths?

The children are using logical reasoning when they are gathering all the available data (i.e. clothing worn, location of party) and deducing the time of year the party was held. This skill continues to be developed throughout their journey in mathematics.

Chapter 19
Painting

Introduction

Exploring colour, shape and texture encourages early mathematical development, and paint is a medium children are familiar with to carry this out. These activities also help children to develop their gross and fine motor skills by using various painting resources to paint on different surfaces.

In your prime

Mix primary colours using ratios to make different hues.

Aims and objectives

- To use ratio.

Resources

- Paints – primary colours only
- Mixing pots
- Teaspoons
- Sugar paper or similar to paint on

Preparation

- You may wish to make your own copy first to show the children.

What to do

- Try mixing different amounts of primary colours. For example:
  a. 4 yellow spoons and 0 red spoons, then
  b. 3 yellow spoons and 1 red spoon, then
  c. 2 yellow spoons and 2 red spoons, then
  d. 1 yellow spoon and 3 red spoons, then
  e. 0 yellow spoons and 4 red spoons.
- Discuss the different shades of orange (or purple or green, depending on the primary colours used) the different recipes make.
- The children can write a recipe for their favourite colour and encourage their friend to copy it and compare the product.

Tips

- **Encourage the children to be as accurate as they can with their teaspoonfuls to gain the best result of the changing hues.**
- **Reinforce language related to ratio, such as three to one (3:1).**

Variation

Use one colour and white or black to create different shades.

How is this maths?

Mixing paints enables young children to begin to explore *ratio* and *proportion*. By creating colours for their friend to copy they begin to learn that *accuracy* is important when *measuring*.

Painting on a large scale

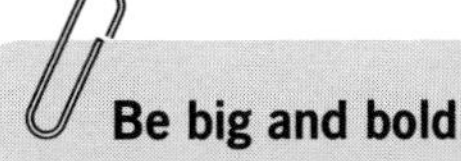

Be big and bold!

Aims and objectives

- To explore large areas in shape and space.

Resources

- Paint – lots of it!
- Big brushes, pads and rollers
- Large items to paint on (see 'What to do' section for ideas)

Preparation

- Ensure there is a space large enough for the activity.

What to do

- Explore large space through painting. Can the children paint the *whole* of the:
  a. sheet of paper on the painting easel?
  b. large box that is being turned into a...?
  c. wall that is being turned into a blackboard area outside (using blackboard paint)?
  d. role-play area's new table?
  e. boulders?

Think big! Try to encourage the children to leave no space unpainted! Be creative in identifying what the children can paint.

Variation

Go elsewhere to paint, such as a gallery or a local secondary school.

How is this maths?

By experiencing large areas and spaces the children are beginning to learn about *scale factors*, *enlargement* and *different sizes*.

Super-small painting

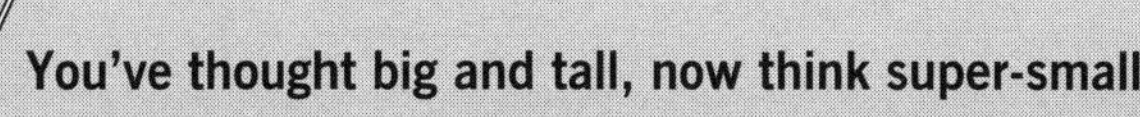

Aims and objectives

- To explore small areas in shape and space.

Resources

- Paint
- Small brushes, pads, sticks and rollers
- Toothpicks
- Small items to paint (see 'What to do' section for ideas)

Preparation

- None required.

What to do

- Explore small space through painting. Can the children paint:
  a. using a very small paintbrush?
  b. their name as small as they can?
  c. using a toothpick on a piece of paper the size of a postage stamp?

Tip **Think small! Use the smallest objects the children can manipulate. Be creative.**

Variation

Paint strawberries with chocolate!

How is this maths?

By experiencing small areas and spaces the children are beginning to learn about *scale factors*, *enlargement* (by less than 0) and different *sizes*.

Chapter 20
The farm

Introduction

Many of the activities in this chapter help children to use their logical thinking skills to group and categorise in a farm context. If possible, a trip to the farm will help the children to see how the farmer keeps the animals healthy by grouping them and keeping them in particular-sized fields. The activities here are related to small-world play but equally could be adapted to a larger space where some of the children become the various animals, looked after by others who are the farmers.

Setting up the farm

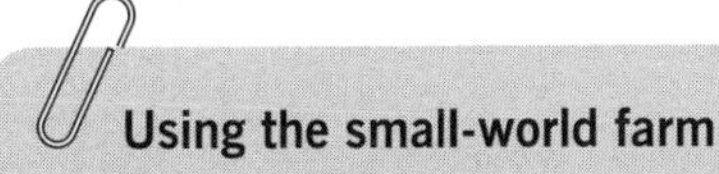

Using the small-world farm.

Aims and objectives

- To practise logical reasoning.
- To learn about estimation.

Resources

- Small-world farm and animals

Preparation

- None required.

What to do

- Ask the children to set up the farm and then leave them alone for a short time.
- Then ask, 'Where is the best place to put the animals? Why did you put the barn there?'
- Discuss the reasons for the decisions made. For example, are the animals that can swim/need water near the pond? Are those that need shelter near trees or a barn? Discuss alternative places the animal could have been placed and why.
- Ask how many particular animals the children estimate there are in the box. Check by counting.
- Ask if the children think that the animals will all fit in a particular pen, or a farm building. Check.

Tip **This develops children's understanding of animals and their needs.**

Variation

Set up other small-world play areas.

How is this maths?

The children are using *estimation* when they are setting up the farm. It is essential that estimation is used in mathematics because it is an excellent way to check the reasonableness of answers when calculations are carried out. Through trial and error the children are also using estimation to develop their understanding of *number* and *counting*. Thinking about alternatives helps to develop a mathematical disposition.

Sorting the animals

Let's help the farmer to sort the animals.

Aims and objectives

- To learn about sorting and categorisation.

Resources

- Farm animals from the small-world area
- Paper to make labels (optional)

Preparation

- None required.

What to do

- Explain to the children that the farmer has decided to farm only one type of animal now, but is not sure what type he should keep. Ask the children to help the farmer by sorting them into types of animals.
- It is likely that the children first sort according to what they are called (e.g. horse). Encourage the children to think about other ways to categorise the animals (e.g. animals with four legs, animals that can fly or animals that lay eggs)
- Are there any categorisations that would mean this farmer had no animals (e.g. wild savannah animals or animals that live in the water)?

Ensure the children have enough space to arrange and rearrange the animals. You may provide paper for them to use so they can create labels for the groups.

Variation

The children can categorise and group everyday objects in a range of ways. Encourage them to be creative and also to identify a category that no objects fit into.

How is this maths?

Sorting leads children into *data handling*. It helps them to understand that *grouping data* can help them to make a big set more manageable. Having items that are going to be the *null set* (such as wild savannah animals in this example) provides an opportunity for children to understand the notion of the *empty set*.

Pens and fences

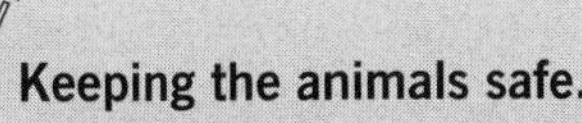

Keeping the animals safe.

Aims and objectives

- To learn about fence length.
- To learn about field area.

Resources

- Fencing and animals from the small-world farm

Preparation

- None required.

What to do

- Ask the children to build fences around the animals to keep them safe.
- Ask, 'How many animals can you fit in the space you have created? Do the animals have everything they need in the space?' Encourage the children to think about overcrowding, shelter, food and water.

Tip **This activity helps the children to think about animal welfare.**

Variation

Think about how much space is needed in different areas of the nursery/ classroom when the children are rearranging a part of it for an activity.

How is this maths?

The children are exploring early *perimeter* (fence length) and *area* (field) in this activity. It will be some time before they are introduced to these formally but here they are intuitively using the ideas. These will develop further as they move through primary school and beyond.

Life cycles

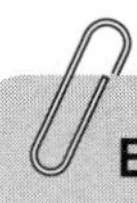

Explore cyclical patterns through animal life cycles.

Aims and objectives

- To identify cyclical patterns.

Resources

- A frog or tadpoles in the nursery/school grounds where the children can observe the life-cycle process
- Butterfly kit or similar

Preparation

- Ensure the area is safe for the children to visit if going to a nature area that is not regularly visited.

What to do

- Observe the tadpoles (or butterfly eggs or other animal) over time. Discuss the changes that the children notice.
- Start to map the cycle to keep a record of what they have seen.
- Eventually talk about how the cycle begins again, making it cyclical.

Tips

- **This activity works well when the children have access to the animal in order to see the life cycle happening themselves.**
- **You can find butterfly kits for sale on the internet or in large garden centres.**

Variation

If no access is possible to live animals or insects, looking at life cycles online, in books or on charts is another way to engage children in the topic.

How is this maths?

Knowing that some patterns are cyclical is an important mathematical notion to understand.

Chapter 21
Parties

Introduction

It is easy to find an excuse to have a party! Perhaps a child's grandparent or an adult in the nursery is reaching a special age, or some of the children in Reception are all turning five at around the same time. However, be aware that some families may not celebrate birthdays or other events as other people do. This is normally related to religious beliefs. If you are in doubt, it would be worth asking the parents or carers about the extent to which they want their child(ren) joining in.

Make wrapping paper

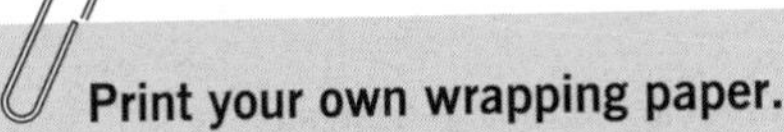

Print your own wrapping paper.

Aims and objectives

- To copy and continue a repeating pattern.
- To create a repeating pattern.

Resources

- Sponges or potatoes for printing
- Paint
- Large sheets of plain newsprint paper for printing on
- Small sheets of paper (about A5) for designing the basic print pattern

Preparation

- You may wish to look at existing wrapping paper and discuss the patterns on the paper and how they continue (repeat). Can the children see how the pattern has been made to repeat? Has it been *slid* along the paper (*translated*), has it been *turned* (*rotated*) and/or has it been *flipped* (*reflected*)?

What to do

- Encourage the children to design a basic print pattern on the small sheets of paper.
- Ask the children to replicate it in one corner of the large plain newsprint paper.
- If necessary, help the children to repeat their pattern.

Tips

- **Check the first design on the A5 paper for the children – are they going to be able to replicate it?**
- **Remember that it doesn't matter if the pattern cannot fit completely onto the large sheet on its last repeat. Patterns continue forever so there should be no white 'border space' around the large sheet either!**
- **Reinforce the language *slide*, *turn* and *flip* as you continue to talk with the children during the activity.**

Variation

Print using a theme such as Hallowe'en, Christmas or Easter.

How is this maths?

The children are exploring geometric patterns using early language related to transformational geometry. They will also begin to understand that patterns have no end and that they keep repeating.

Wrap the parcel

Prepare together for the traditional party game.

Aims and objectives

- To use vocabulary related to large and small.
- To understand surface area.

Resources

- A small gift already wrapped so the children do not know what it is
- A number of sheets of wrapping paper piled so that the largest sheet is on the bottom and the smallest is on the top
- Sticky tape
- Scissors

Preparation

- Ensure the gift for the middle of the parcel is already wrapped once.

What to do

- Check all the children know how to play pass the parcel.
- Explain that they will all be preparing for the game now, and then they will play it at a later date.
- Place the pile of paper on the floor in the middle of the circle. Ask the children what they notice about the pile of paper in the centre. Discuss the different sizes and how the paper is piled with the *largest* at the bottom and the *smallest* at the top. Ask the children if they know why you might have done that.
- Pass the parcel to different children and ask them to wrap the gift.
- Talk about the relative size of the parcel and how it is changing, becoming *bigger* and *bigger* as it is wrapped.

Tips

- **Because the children are wrapping the parcel themselves, ensure the gift is particularly small and that there is a lot of room for growth in the pre-prepared papers.**
- **Some children may become confused because they normally *unwrap* the parcel. You may need to explain several times that the children are preparing for the game. Asking children to come to you to wrap the parcel may avoid the confusion that passing the parcel around the circle could bring.**

Variation

Although it may not look as attractive, newspaper works just as well in developing children's understanding of the concepts and it helps you to recycle previously used paper!

How is this maths?

By preparing for the game the children are exploring very early notions of *inverse operations* – what started small becomes *bigger* and will then become *smaller* again as it is unwrapped. This is fundamentally what happens with addition and subtraction, and multiplication and division being inverse operations. Early notions of *surface area* are also explored by noticing that the paper needs to become bigger as the parcel also becomes bigger.

Pass the parcel

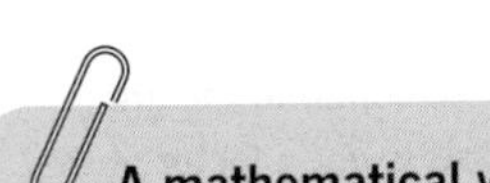

A mathematical variation on the traditional game.

Aims and objectives

- To learn about taking turns.
- To practise counting.
- To use vocabulary related to large and small.

Resources

- The parcel made earlier by the children
- Large bin liner

Preparation

- If the children have not collaboratively wrapped the parcel you will need to create one by wrapping a small gift in several separate layers of paper.
- If the children did prepare it, you may need to add more layers before the game is played.

What to do

- Identify a child to start.
- Pass the parcel around the circle but instead of using music count to a given number, say 9, and pass on each count.
- When the ninth person receives the parcel they unwrap one layer.
- Counting starts again from 1 and the parcel is passed around again.
- When the ninth person receives the parcel they unwrap one layer.
- When several people have unwrapped a layer it may be that a child gets the parcel again.
- If there are some children who have not unwrapped the parcel yet continue to move the parcel, without counting, to the next child who is yet to unwrap.
- Start counting from 1 again.
- Once everyone has had a go unwrapping then give children the opportunity for a second turn.

Tips

- **Ask another adult to go to each child unwrapping the parcel and collect the used paper in a bin liner.**
- **To make the game flow, count the number of children in the group and select a number to count to each time that is *not* a factor of that number.**

Variation

You could play the traditional game where the children pass the parcel around the circle until you pause the music.

How is this maths?

The children are practising their counting skills. They are also being involved in a numerical pattern that develops around the circle. Using music helps children to follow directions.

Wrap that box

A game that involves wrapping boxes.

Aims and objectives

- To match boxes with wrapping paper.

Resources

- A number of boxes, all of varying sizes
- A number of sheets of paper, all different sizes
- Sticky tape

Preparation

- Check that the sheets of paper will each wrap one of the boxes snugly. Make a note for yourself as to which paper matches each box most appropriately.

What to do

- Divide the group into two teams and sit them facing each other on a large carpet area.
- Line the sheets of paper in size order on the floor between the two teams.
- Display the boxes in an arbitrary way at one end.
- Ask for a volunteer from one team to select one box.
- Encourage the team to offer suggestions as to the paper that would wrap it best.
- The volunteer places it on one sheet of paper. (Once the paper has been touched the child is unable to change their mind!)
- They check that it is the best fit. If they are correct their team scores one point.
- It is now the other team's turn.
- If a team is incorrect (as the adult who has checked beforehand you will know which one is the best fit) the box is passed to the other team to try.
- The game continues until all the boxes have been covered. The winning team is the team with the highest score.

Tip

You may want to demonstrate before the game starts what an appropriate fit is, to avoid confusion later on.

Variation

Use paper that matches a particular theme, for example birthday party wrapping paper for parties and Christmas paper in December.

How is this maths?

Early notions of surface area are explored in this game, by matching paper to boxes.

Guess the present

Time to be creative and have some fun guessing what could be in the box!

Aims and objectives

- To visualise size and shape.
- To understand volume.

Resources

- A number of empty wrapped boxes, all different sizes and shapes

Preparation

- The boxes may have been wrapped in the previous activity, or you may need/want to set up a different set of boxes of varying shapes (including, say, a basketball shape or a triangular Toblerone box).

What to do

- The children pass one wrapped empty box around. Before they pass it to the next child they must state one item that could be in the box. The item that 'could' be in the box may be nonsense (e.g. a jellyfish) but they cannot pass the box until they have identified something that could actually fit in the box (i.e. they could not say 'house').
- Pass around different-sized and -shaped boxes.

Tips

- **You do not have to pass the same box right around the circle if there is a large group of children.**
- **Encourage the children to be as creative as they can.**

Variation

Instead of boxes, pass around different sticks and the children have to state an object that is about the same height as the stick.

How is this maths?

This is a fun way for children to visualise the *volume* of boxes.

Birthday cards and candles

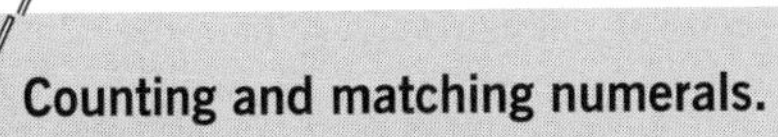

Counting and matching numerals.

Aims and objectives

- To practise counting.
- To recognise numbers.

Resources

- Selection of toys (with names displayed if the children are not familiar with their names)
- A number of birthday cards with different ages on them, each written out to a different toy
- A polystyrene cylinder painted to look like a birthday cake (or a role-play cake that has holes for candles, or a real cake the children can share later!)
- Small birthday candles with holders
- Lighter (for an adult only) to light the candles

Preparation

- Painting the cake takes some time if you go for that option!

What to do

- Explain to the children that today is the birthday of several of the toys in the nursery/class.
- Pass the toys out for different children to hold and remind the children of their names.
- Show the children the envelope/card for one of the toys and ask one child to open it.
- Deduce that the toy is turning the number that is on the card.
- Suggest that the children sing the toy 'Happy Birthday' and give them a cake with candles.
- Show the children the cake and select one child to push the correct number of candles into the cake, counting as they go.

- Light the candles (if appropriate to do so) and ask the children to join in singing 'Happy Birthday' to the toy while you are moving towards the toy and small group of children who will blow the candles out.

Tips

- **If necessary, check on your centre/school policy about lighting candles and children blowing them out. Take appropriate precautions to ensure all the children remain safe and are not in danger of being burnt.**
- **Remind the children of the need to stay where they are in the circle and ensure the children know who is going to blow the candles out. Reassure the children that they will all get a turn.**

Variation

Unwrap a little present for the toy that the children can share.

How is this maths?

The children are reading the number on the card and counting out the corresponding number of candles.

You're invited!

Design invitations for friends and family, toys or other children to come to the party!

Aims and objectives

- To use a range of time-related measurements.

Resources

- Blank paper or invitation templates

Preparation

- Prepare invitation templates, if using, to include:
  a. Whom it is addressed to.
  b. Where the party is.
  c. When (date and time).
  d. Why (purpose of party: whose birthday is it and how old are they going to be?)

What to do

- Using the template or blank paper the children design their own birthday party invitations for a special guest.

Tips

- **Vary the amount you have completed the template depending on the children's confidence or motivation in writing.**
- **Encourage the children to draw pictures if this is more appropriate.**

Variation

Make a whole-class invitation to invite a neighbouring class of children to a party. Construct parts of the invitation in shared writing time and then, during guided group work, encourage children to decorate the invitation and write the name on it.

How is this maths?

The who, where, when and why questions are often used in data-handling cycles to gather data and answer questions. Measurement of time uses many different *units* and *bases*. Here the time of the party (analogue time and date) and the age of the child (in years) are used.

Chapter 22
Let's make music

Introduction

Music and mathematics are very closely related. These activities explore the relationship between the two subjects. You can involve all the children together in these activities, or they can be planned as an adult-led activity for a small group of children. Leaving instruments available for children to use during continuous provision can emphasise ideas explored together previously, or offer children the opportunity to develop their own rhythms and patterns. Encouraging them to record and play back their compositions helps to reinforce intuitive structure and pattern in music.

Count the beat

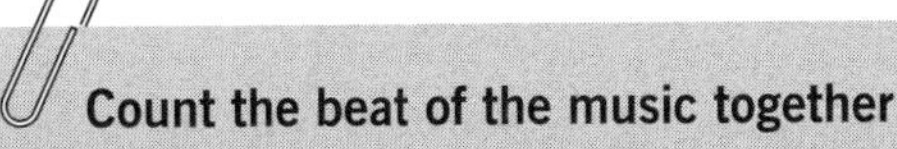

Count the beat of the music together.

Aims and objectives

- To practise counting.
- To learn about pattern.

Resources

- Percussion instruments – one per child

Preparation

- None required.

What to do

- Hand out the instruments to the children in the group.
- Encourage the children to count as they play the instrument to match the beat (1, 2, 3, 4, 1, 2, 3, 4, 1, 2, 3, 4 and so on).
- Divide the children into two groups. Alternate the groups so, while group A is playing four beats group B is resting (not playing their instruments) for four beats. Then, keeping the beat, group B plays for four beats while group A rests.
- Divide the class into four groups. The children will play four beats when you are pointing to their group but will rest (not play) when another group is being pointed to.

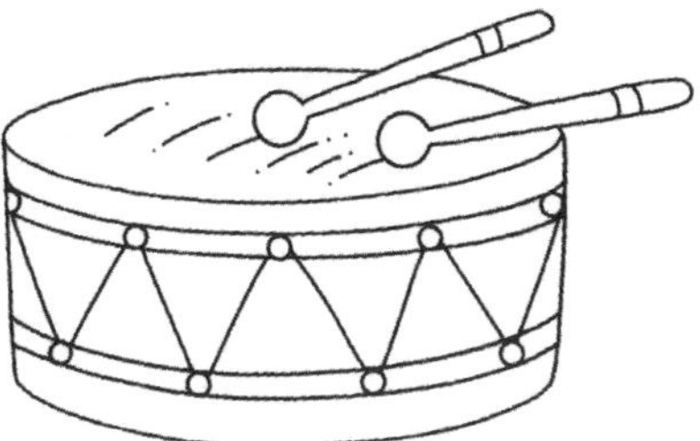

Tip

Ask a child to be the conductor after you have modelled the role for a while and you have identified a child that might be able to lead the class in the counting and playing.

Variations

- Try a different beat – what about a waltz? 1, 2, 3, 1, 2, 3, 1, 2, 3 and so on. Put an emphasis on the first beat of each bar.
- Encourage the children to play the rhythm of a favourite song while they count out the beats (this is challenging!).

How is this maths?

Counting the beat and continuing the pattern develops an understanding of structure. Structure is important in mathematics, music and poetry, to name just three examples.

I got rhythm!

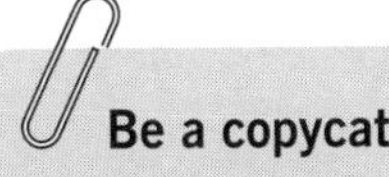

Be a copycat.

Aims and objectives

- To copy and continue patterns.

Resources

- Percussion instruments – one per child (optional as the children can simply clap the rhythm)

Preparation

- None required.

What to do

- Clap or play a short rhythm for the children to repeat like an echo.
- Repeat the rhythm for the children to copy.
- When you and the children are ready, change the rhythm.

Tip **When first following rhythms the children may find it easier to clap rather than play instruments.**

Variation

Identify a child who can lead the children in this activity.

How is this maths?

Music, no matter how simple or complex, follows structures that are intuitively pleasing. Later on the children will learn to use musical notation to record the music. Musical notation uses a lot of mathematics – for example, fractions are used to identify the length of notes.

Exploring sounds

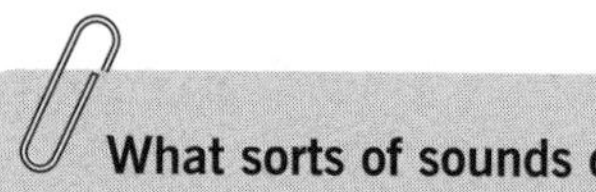

What sorts of sounds can be made?

Aims and objectives

- To learn about duration.
- To understand pitch.

Resources

- A selection of musical instruments that can play at least two pitches – one per child

Preparation

- None required.

What to do

- Ask the children the following questions. 'Can you make:
  a. *Long* sounds? *Short* sounds?
  b. *Loud* sounds? *Quiet* sounds?
  c. *High* sounds? *Low* sounds?
  d. *Fast* sounds? *Slow* sounds?'

Tip **Encourage the children to make a different type of sound once they have tried one way.**

Variation

Instead of using instruments play music that represents the aspects identified above. Encourage the children to use body movement to reflect the sounds. For example, the children might use big movements to represent loud and very small movements to represent quiet. Talk about why they are moving in their chosen ways.

How is this maths?

Thinking about producing a type of sound in another way encourages children to be creative. Being creative in mathematics is important because it helps people to solve problems using different approaches. Duration involves identifying length of time, perhaps intuitively or by counting beats. The passing of time is also a mathematical notion.

Chapter 23
The bakery

Introduction

Although local bakeries are becoming fewer in number, you may be fortunate to be close enough for the children to visit one to spark off the ideas in this chapter's theme. Alternatively, you could invite a parent or friend who bakes bread or cakes at home to talk to the children about baking. Many of the activities will need to be undertaken with more adult support than others in this book, so you may want to enlist the help of parents for a baking day, or arrange for small groups of children to take turns over a week. Setting up a bakery in the role-play area offers children an opportunity to assume the role of a baker without the need to be precise in measurements or to work with a hot oven. If you have space you may set up the bakery next to the café (see Chapter 16) so that goodies can be supplied.

Baking

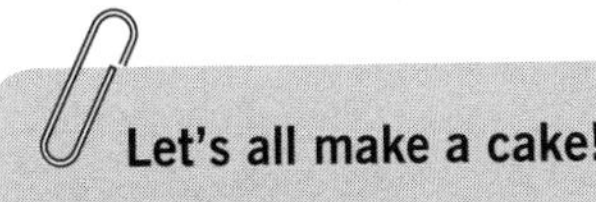

Let's all make a cake!

Aims and objectives

- To learn about measurement.

Resources

- Cake recipe
- Ingredients
- Measuring equipment such as weighing scales and measuring cups

Preparation

- Ensure the oven is working and available if the recipe requires cooking.

What to do

- Read through the recipe with the children.
- Follow the recipe by:
  a. Helping the children to *weigh* the ingredients.
  b. *Counting* the number of eggs.
  c. Mixing for a given length of *time*.
  d. Identifying what *temperature* the cake needs to be cooked at.
  e. Setting a *timer* according to how long the cake needs to be in the oven.

Reinforce the mathematical language related to measurement when you speak with the children. Encourage them to use appropriate vocabulary throughout the baking process.

Variation

You may make a different item with different groups so you can have a party at the end of the day with the different goodies.

How is this maths?

The children are using a number of different units of measurement in a meaningful context, for example grams or kilograms, minutes or hours and degrees Celsius.

Sharing evenly

If we are sharing our baking, how many will we get each?

Aims and objectives

- To understand division as sharing evenly.
- To understand division as grouping.

Resources

- The cooked items, or pictures/counters to represent them

Preparation

- None required.

What to do

- Ask the children to identify how many items are being made, or have been made.
- Ask the children to identify how many people the items are going to be shared between.
- Talk about strategies for sharing the items evenly.

Tip

If there are several items and few children then encourage them to share out the items more than one at a time because it speeds up the process. This is division by grouping.

Variation

Have a range of items that need to be shared.

How is this maths?

Division by sharing often develops into division by grouping. This progression helps children to understand what division (as a concept) means and helps them to understand more formal methods of division later on.

The cup-cake problem

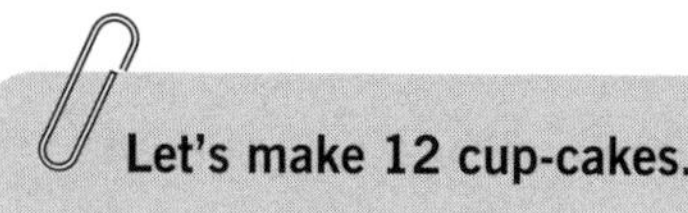

Let's make 12 cup-cakes.

Aims and objectives

- To practise addition.
- To practise subtraction.

Resources

- One muffin tray
- 12 (real or role-play) cup-cakes

Preparation

- None required.

What to do

- Explain to the children that we need 12 cup-cakes.
- Show the tray with six cup-cakes in it.
- Ask, 'How many more cup-cakes do we need?'.
- Encourage the children to talk to each other to share their answers and ways of working it out with each other.
- Repeat for other numbers of cupcakes on the tray.
- You may wish to model the number sentence on the board.

Tips

- **Encourage the children to decide how many cup-cakes will be in the tray to start the next time. They will be responsible for leading the discussion afterwards about the answer and checking if it is correct.**
- **Remember to include starting with no (0) cup-cakes and 12 cup-cakes at some stage.**

Variation

Use different contexts, such as eggs in an egg carton (boil them for longevity!).

How is this maths?

Some of the children will simply count the remaining spaces. This is finding the answer through using *addition by counting on*. Others will see the problem as a *subtraction* where they find the *difference by counting on*. Some children may just know the answer through visualisation or familiarisation with *number bonds* to 12.

Use your loaf!

Observe the effect yeast has during the bread-making process.

Aims and objectives

- To describe enlargement.
- To measure the passing of time.

Resources

- Simple bread-making recipe with ingredients or a packet of bread mix
- Plastic sheeting
- Large bowl
- Cling film
- Butter for spreading on the bread when it is baked
- Knife for spreading the butter

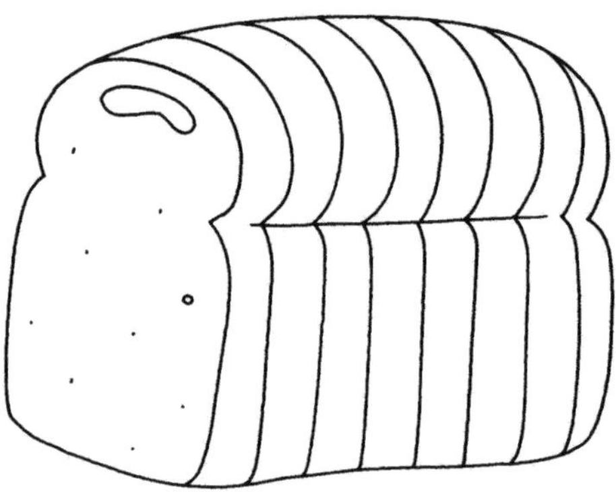

Preparation

- Check the oven is available and working at the time you will be baking your bread.
- Scrub down the kneading surface so that it is spotless.

What to do

- Ensure the children wash their hands well prior to starting.
- Follow the bread recipe, ensuring plenty of kneading and raising time is allowed for.
- Give the children the opportunity to see the dough before it is left to rise and after the allotted time.
- Discuss the change and the active ingredient that caused it – yeast. Share with the children that the yeast lets off a gas called carbon dioxide during the resting period (fermentation) and the gas causes the dough to *increase* in size.
- Bake according to the recipe.

Tip

Bread mixes are very easy to use because they include all the ingredients you require and you simply add water (but have a little more flour on standby in case the dough becomes too sticky). However, you miss out on the opportunity for the children to feel, smell and measure the individual ingredients separately, particularly the active ingredient, yeast. Perhaps have some more yeast available separately so this can be seen and touched by the children, while the bread mix is used to make the bread.

Variation

There are many types of bread that you can make quite simply to celebrate different festivals. Select an appropriate recipe for the time of year.

How is this maths?

The yeast has a profound effect on the dough. Looking at how the dough has risen is related to shape and space and specifically *enlargement*. There is a lot of waiting during the bread-making process. This *passing of time* is measured using timers or by reading the time on the clock.

Five currant buns

Singing songs related to baking helps us to understand number.

Aims and objectives

- To count backwards.
- To take away one at a time.

Resources

- Backing music (optional)
- Five currant buns from the role-play area or five laminated pictures of currant buns that can be attached to the wall and easily removed.

Preparation

- If you are not sure of the tune, find the song using an internet search of the first line of the lyrics.
- Set up the currant buns on a plate or stick the pictures to the board.

What to do

- Start singing the song (see lyrics below). Where there is a gap in the lyrics, name one child from the group to take a bun at the appropriate moment in the song.
- Keep singing until all the buns are gone.

Lyrics

Five currant buns in a baker's shop.
Big and round with a cherry on the top,
Along came ________ with a penny one day,
Bought a currant bun and took it away.
Four currant buns...
Three...
Two...
One...

You may want to place the numerals 1–5 on the buns to help the children learn to read the numbers.

Variations

- Start and end the song at any number you wish! Do not be constrained by starting with 'five' each time.
- Choose the children's favourite baked items and substitute them in the song, for example 'pitta bread', 'crusty loaves' or 'hot cross buns'.

How is this maths?

Counting backwards is an early entry into *subtraction* and *taking away* one. Knowing that no currant buns exist helps children understand that it is possible to count backwards to zero, but that we begin at one when we start counting.

The role-play bakery

Are the children master bakers?

Aims and objectives

- To learn about measurement.
- To practise division.

Resources

- The role-play area set up as a bakery
- Ingredients for measuring such as raisins or flour
- Scales
- Bowls
- Play dough (see recipe on page 229) or real flour dough
- Buns, loaves, pies and pastries
- A brush and shovel!

Preparation

- The children may have visited a local bakery to learn what goes on there so they can develop the role play area further themselves.

What to do

There are many activities that can be undertaken in the bakery role play. These include:

- Measuring and weighing specific quantities.
- Kneading the play dough or real bread dough.
- Plaiting the play dough or real bread dough.
- Dividing the cake mixture evenly.
- Selling and buying bread and other goods.

Tips

- **Remind the children they cannot eat the play dough!**
- **Real loaves and buns can be preserved by varnishing them two or three times, leaving a drying period between each coat. (Again, remind they are not to be eaten.)**

Variation

The role-play area can be a corner shop selling baking ingredients and baked items.

How is this maths?

In the role play area the children can enact most of the tasks that bakers carry out. *Measuring* ingredients is a necessary skill to master. *Dividing* mixture in order to make evenly sized cup-cakes or loaves is another. Plaiting the dough requires the children to be *systematic*.

Appendices

References

Books

Freedman, Claire and Cort, Ben, *Aliens Love Underpants*, London: Simon and Schuster Children's, 2007

Harris, Peter and Allwright, Deborah, *The Night Pirates*, London: Egmont Books Ltd, 2005

Helbrough, Emma and Gower, Teri, *1001 Bugs to Spot*, London: Usborne Books, 2009

King, Valerie, *In Comes the Tide*, Loughborough: Ladybird Books Ltd, 1997

Manning, Mick and Granstrom, Brita, *High Tide, Low Tide*, London: Franklin Watts, 2003

Mitton, Tony and Young, Selina, *Once Upon a Tide*, London: Picture Corgi, 2006

Pfister, Marcus, *The Rainbow Fish*, New York: NorthSouth Books, 2007

Punter, Russell and Fox, Christyan, *Stories of Pirates*, London: Usborne Books, 2007

Thomson, Emma, *Lili's Wish*, London: Orchard Books, 2007

Music

Vivaldi, Antonio, *The Four Seasons*, 1723 (numerous editions)

Index of activities

Activity	Page number
Communication, Language and Literacy	
Language for Communication	
Aliens	35
Nothing but net	49
The doll's house	98
Pairs	124
Golden eggs	191
You're invited!	279
The cup-cake problem	294
Language for Thinking	
Go Fish!	43
Snakes and ladders	58
Types of shoes	118
Boxes	121
Guess who?	122
Treasure chest	163
A pirate investigation	165
I choose that glass	219
Reading	
Retelling Jack and the Beanstalk	193
Garçon, I'd like to order please	215
Mixing drinks	218
Baking	291
Writing	
Message in a bottle	161
May I take your order now?	216
Handwriting	
Drawing a tower	204
Decorating biscuits	221

Activity	Page number
Sequences and Pattern	
Making necklaces	7
Day and night	32
Retelling Jack and the Beanstalk	193
The four seasons	246
Celebrating through the seasons	247
I got rhythm!	285
Measurement	
Shoe sizes	117
Calculating	
Pattern	
The tide	18
Adding and Taking Away	
Spacemen	33
Nothing but net	49
Floor robot games	60
Beanbags	63
Hide-and-count	65
Make a group	66
Making the sandwiches	108
One elephant came out to play	133
Golden eggs	191
The cup-cake problem	294
Division	
Treasure chest	163
Sharing evenly	293
Problem-solving	
Guess who?	122
A pirate investigation	165
Wind	241
Shadows	243
In your prime	251
Setting up the farm	259
The role-play bakery	300
Shape, Space and Measures	
Shape and Space	
Other people's homes	85
A nonsense house	86
Making dens	88
Shapely sandwiches	110
I'm a circle	139
The farm is shaping up	141
Shape hunt	151

Activity	Page number
Time	
Time for the picnic?	105
Create your own shadows	244
Life cycles	264
You're invited!	278
Exploring sounds	286
Ordering	
My feet	115
Order! Order!	175
Let's harp on about it	189
Being tall	208
Size	
As small as small can be	147
Making things bigger	177
Investigating small creatures	179
Create something big!	182
One small step for Jack, one giant step outside!	197
Drawing a tower	204
Painting on a large scale	253
Super-small painting	255
Guess the present	274
Capacity	
I choose that glass	219
Wrap the parcel	269
Wrap that box	273
Grouping and Sorting	
In the clothes shop	3
The rock pool	20
Travelling	77
My day	80
Types of shoes	118
Boxes	121
Colour	154
Texture	156
Our weather station	239
Sorting the animals	261
Problem-solving	
Tall tower competition	201
Thinking about towers	206
Lock her in the tower!	209

Activity	Page number
Place	
The rock pool	20
To infinity and beyond!	27
Spacemen	33
My home	92
A living treasure island	159
Treasure maps	160
Climb the beanstalk	195
Thinking about towers	206
The four seasons	246
Communities	
That's just up our street!	90
The tables	213
Physical Development	
Movement and Space	
The tide	18
Fish race	45
Beanbags	63
Travelling	77
Air finger-numbers	227
Making big numbers	232
Health and Bodily Awareness	
I've caught a big one!	41
My body	75
My day	80
My feet	115
Being tall	208
Using Equipment and Materials	
Beach towels	16
Rocket construction	26
Making the sandwiches	108
Shapely sandwiches	110
It's a wrap!	111
Have you got sole?	126
Order! Order!	175